KT-134-872

THE GIANT PICTURE DICTIONARY FOR BOYS AND GIRLS

by ALICE HOWARD SCOTT, M.A.

illustrated by
ANNA CAMESAS and MARY JUNGBECK

© Peter Haddock Ltd, Bridlington
England

FOREWORD

In recent years the world has become reading-conscious. It has always recognised the necessity of mastering the three R's, but today more than at any time in the history of the world, there is widespread acceptance of the fact that boys and girls, men and women, should be able to read efficiently. The most important of the three R's is reading.

No progress can be made in reading efficiently without word mastery. The sooner boys and girls become accustomed to the use of the dictionary, the greater will be their ability to cope with new words. The GIANT PICTURE DICTIONARY FOR BOYS AND GIRLS is designed to help them establish the dictionary habit in the early years. The definitions of the words reflect current thinking.

This dictionary will serve as a reading text as well as a dictionary. The attractive format, the lively artistic illustrations, as well as the challenging vocabulary, make the GIANT PICTURE DICTIONARY FOR BOYS AND GIRLS an absorbing interest in the study of words, and make learning an adventure.

THE GIANT PICTURE DICTIONARY FOR BOYS AND GIRLS

A a

a, an

A cat is **an** animal.
Use **an before a, e, i, o, u.**

abandon

The ship was sinking.
The captain gave the order to **abandon** ship.
The men left the ship.

abbreviation

An **abbreviation** is a short way to write a word.
A full-stop is put after most **abbreviations. abbr**.

ability

Jane has **ability** in reading.
Jane can read very well.

able

Baby is **able** to walk.
Baby can walk.

aboard

The sailor is **aboard** ship.
He is on the ship.
The conductor called, "All **aboard**!"
All passengers went into the train.
Then the train started.

about

Read us the story **about** Peter Rabbit.
Peter is in the story.

above

There is a picture **above** my bed.
Above means over.

abroad

Father has been **abroad**.
Father has been in other countries.

absence

During my **absence**, we had a visitor.
He came when I was away.

A

B C D E F G H I J K L M N O P Q R S T U V W X Y Z

absent

Helen was **absent** Friday.
She was not here Friday.

abundance, abundant

We have an **abundance** of food.
We have **abundant** food.
We have more than enough.

accept

Dot asked me to her party.
I shall **accept** the invitation.
I shall say that I
shall be glad to come.

accident

Ralph had an **accident**.
He fell downstairs.

account

1. Mother keeps an **account.**
She writes down the amount
of money she receives,
the amount she spends,
and the amount that is left.
2. Dad gave an **account**
of his trip abroad.
He told the story of his trip.

ace, aces

1. An **ace** is as expert.
The best players of baseball
are called baseball **aces.**
2. These cards are **aces.**
Each card has one spot.

ache, aching, aches

An **ache** is a pain that
goes on and on.
My ear is **aching.**
When my ear **aches,**
I go to see the doctor.

acorn

An **acorn** is
the seed of
an oak tree.

acquaintance

Jane is my **acquaintance.**
I know her, but not well.

acquire

Jim hopes to **acquire** a
watch.
He hopes to get a watch.

admiral

An **admiral** is a high
officer in the navy.

admire

We **admire**
the picture
that Helen has painted.
We think that it is very good.

admission

Admission to the movie
is thirty-five pence.
It costs that much to go in.

admit

One ticket will
admit you
to our
circus.
One ticket will let you in.

adult

An **adult** is
a grown-up
person.

advance

The cars **advance** slowly
on the narrrow road.
They go forward slowly.

advantage

A safety pin has an
advantage over a
straight pin.
A safety pin is better.
It is safer to use.
The point can be fastened.
Then it cannot scratch you.

adventure

An **adventure**
is an unusual event.
Pete had an aeroplane ride.
That was an **adventure.**

advertise, advertisement

People
advertise things to sell.
An **advertisement** is a
notice about things to
buy or sell.

A B C D E F G H I J K L M N O P Q R S T U V W X Y Z

advice, advise

I need your **advice.**
How would you **advise** me?
What do you think
I ought to do?

affair

Tom and Ann had a quarrel.
It was not my **affair.**
It was not a matter
in which I had a part.

affect

Will the rain **affect** your plans?
Will it change your plans?

affection, affectionate

Virginia
shows
affection.
She is
affectionate.
She is loving.

afford

Dad cannot **afford** to buy it.
He has not enough money.

afire

The house
is **afire.**
It is
burning.

afraid

Jenny is **afraid**
of Spot.
She thinks
that he
will
hurt her.

after

1. B comes **after** A.
A comes first.
B comes next.
2. We play **after** school.
We play when school is over.

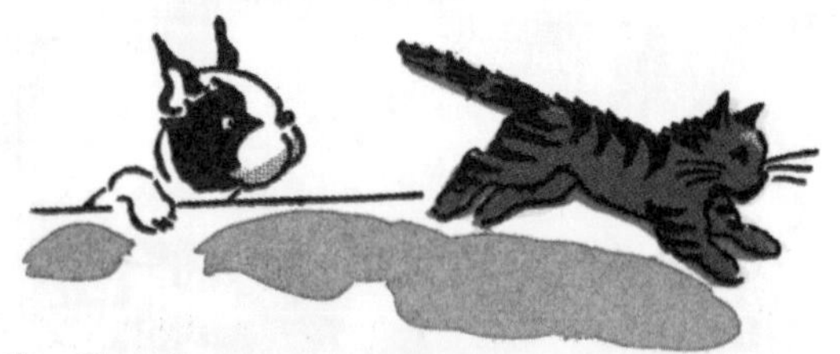

3. Spot ran **after** the cat.
Spot was chasing the cat.

afternoon

We shopped all **afternoon.**
We shopped from the middle
of the day until evening.

afterwards

Susy had a nap. **Afterwards**
she had ice cream.
She had ice cream later.

again

Sing the song **again.**
Sing it one more time.

against

1. The ladder
   is **against** the wall.
It leans on the wall.
2. We walk
   against
   the wind.
   We walk into the wind.

age

Martin's **age** is eight.
Martin is eight years old.

agent

An **agent** came to see us.
He worked for a company.
He was selling books.

ago

Years **ago**, there were
no automobiles.
In past years, people
had horses and carriages.

agree

Dick and John **agree** that
our team played well.
They both think that our
team played well.

ahead

Look **ahead** when you walk.
Look to the front.

aid, aids

I **aid** mother.
Ann **aids**
her, too.
We help her.

aim, aimed

Tony's **aim** is bad.
He **aimed** the ball at Jim,
but he hit the window.

air

Air is all
around us.
We cannot
see it.
We can feel it
when we
are near
the fan.
We breathe **air.**
We pump **air** into tyres.

airedale

Ted's dog is
an **airedale**.

also

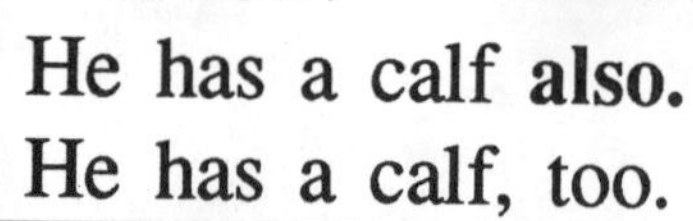

Edward has
a cow.
He has a calf **also.**
He has a calf, too.

altar

An **altar** is a kind of table
used in a place of worship.

alter

Rose's dress does not fit.
She will **alter** it.
She will change it.

although

Although he is tired,
Jack has to mow the lawn.
Even if he is tired, Jack
has to mow the lawn.

altogether

1. **Altogether**, we saw
ten different birds.
Counting all, we saw
ten different birds.
2. John has **altogether**
forgotten his lesson.
He has forgotten it completely.

always

Joe's dog is **always** friendly.
He is friendly at all times.

am, are, is

Beth says, "I **am** a teacher.
You **are** the pupils.
Scrappy **is** a visitor."

ambition

Richard's **ambition**
is to be a doctor.
He hopes to be a doctor
when he is older.

among

There are green berries **among** the ripe ones.
There are green berries mixed with the ripe ones.

amount

Edward bought groceries.
The **amount** he paid was £2.40.

amuse

Susy can **amuse** herself with her blocks.
She has fun.

amusement

The **amusement** park has many things to enjoy.

anchor

The anchor holds the ship in place.

ancient

This redwood is an **ancient** tree.
It is 1000 years old.

and

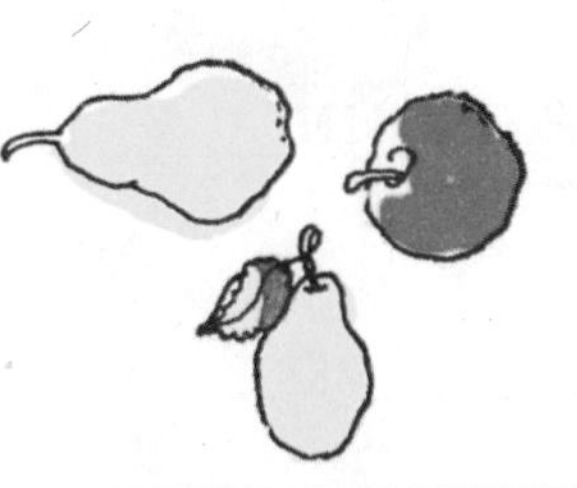

Here is a pear.
Here are a pear **and** an apple.

angel

1. An **angel** is a messenger of God.
2. An **angel** is very good and kind.

angle

An **angle** is the space between two straight lines that meet at a point.

angry

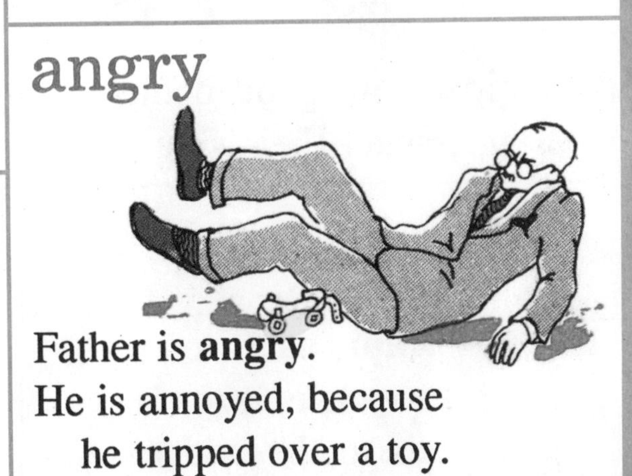

Father is **angry**.
He is annoyed, because he tripped over a toy.

A B C D E F G H I J K L M N O P Q R S T U V W X Y Z

A

B C D E F G H I J K L M N O P Q R S T U V W X Y Z

applaud, applause

The people will **applaud.**
They will clap their hands.
We can hear the **applause.**
People like the song.

apple

An **apple** is a fruit.

apply, applying, applied

Jim will **apply** for a job.
He will ask to have it.
He is **applying** in two places.
He **applied** for another job.

appoint

The teacher will **appoint** Dick to be librarian.
Dick will be given that position.

appreciate

We **appreciate** good books.
We understand their value.

approach

This is an **approach** to the bridge. It is a road that leads to the bridge.

approve

Aunt Mary does not **approve** of lazy boys.
She thinks it is wrong to be lazy.

apricot

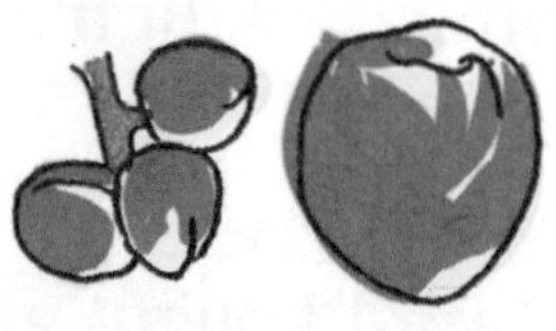

An **apricot** is a fruit.
It is smaller than a peach.

apron

Mary wears an **apron** to keep her dress clean while she is working.

apt

1. Tom is **apt** to forget.
He often forgets.
2. Jane is an **apt** pupil.
She learns quickly.

arch, arches

An **arch** is curved.

Two **arches** support the bridge.

art, artist

Painting is an **art.**
Making statues is an **art.**
Those things take skill.
The **artist** is painting a picture.

as

The cat's fur is **as** soft **as** velvet.
The cat's fur and velvet are equally soft.

ascend

We **ascend** the hill.
We go up the hill.

ashamed

Pal stole meat.
He is **ashamed.**
He knows that he did wrong.

ashes

Fire has burned the wood.
Only **ashes** are left.

aside

Toby was not hit.
The car turned **aside.**
It turned to one side.

ask

Why does the snow fall?
When I wish to know something, I **ask** a question.

asleep

Baby is **asleep.**

assembly, assemblies

We have **assembly** at school.
All the children meet in one room. We have plays at our **assemblies.**

assign, assignment

The teacher will **assign** words for us to study.
She will give us an **assignment.**
She will give us work to do.

assist, assistance

The Scout offered to **assist** the lady.
He offered **assistance**.
He offered to help her.

assistant

Pete is Jim's **assistant.**
He helps Jim deliver papers.

aster

The **aster** is a flower.
The **aster** grows in fields or gardens.

astonish

The big trees of California will **astonish** you.
They will surprise you.
They will fill you with wonder.

at

We were not **at** home today.
We were not in the house.

athlete

Jerry is an **athlete**.
He is strong and good in sports.

atmosphere

The **atmosphere** is a blanket of air.
It covers the earth.

atom, atoms, atomic

An **atom** is too tiny to be seen.
Everything is made of **atoms**.
By breaking the **atom,** we can get **atomic** power.

attach

We are going to **attach** the tail to our kite.
We shall fasten it on.

attack

1. Our army will **attack.**
   Our army will make the first move against the enemy.
2. Jane had an **attack** of measles. She was sick.

attempt

Paul made an **attempt** to climb the tree.
He tried to climb it.

attend, attendance

1. **Attend** to the speaker.
   Listen to the speaker.
2. We **attend** a good school.

We go to a good school.
Allison had perfect **attendance** at school.
She went to school every day this term.

attention, attentive

Dick is not paying **attention** to the reading lesson.
He is not **attentive.**
He is thinking about a baseball game.

attic

The **attic** is a room just under the roof.

attract

Sugar will **attract** flies.
Sugar makes flies come.

audience

Our circus had an **audience.**
Five children came to see it.

aunt

Aunt Edith is my father's sister.
Aunt Emma is my mother's sister.

author

An **author** is a person who writes books.

autograph

Helen has the author's **autograph.** He wrote his name in her book.

automatic

Mary's house has an **automatic** lift.
It does not need a lift boy to run it.

automobile

An **automobile** is a vehicle.
It is run by a motor.
Dad drives a green **automobile.**

autumn

Autumn is the season between summer and winter.

avenue

Joe lives on Terrace **Avenue.**
It is a wide street.

average

1. Jack is an **average** boy.
   He is like most boys.
2. His marks in arithmetic are 70% and 80%.
   His **average** is 75%.

aviation

Bob studies **aviation.**
He learns about aeroplanes and flying.

aviator

An **aviator** is a flier.

avoid

Joan has a cold.
She tries to **avoid** other people.
She stays away from them.

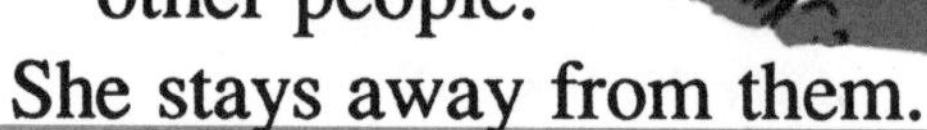

await

It is Tom's birthday.
A surprise may **await** him.
He may find a present waiting for him.

awake, awoke

Baby is not asleep.
He is wide **awake.**
He **awoke** early.

away

Daddy is going **away.**
He will go many miles
from home.

awful

Harry had an **awful**
dream.
It was a very bad dream.

awhile

We played tag for **awhile.**
We played for a short time.

axe, axes

This is an
axe.
Men use
axes to
chop down trees.

axis

The earth turns on its **axis.**
This globe
turns on an
axis, too.

axle

The wheels of Paul's cart are
on an **axle.**

B b

baa

The sheep says **baa.**

baby, babies

Mother is
feeding **baby.**
Babies are
very young.
They need
our care.

back

The chipmunk
has a stripe on
his **back.**

Baby is lying
on his **back.**
There is a
small
porch at
the **back** of the house.

backward

May dressed
herself.
She put her
dress on
backward.
The back is in front.

bacon

Bacon is cured meat.
We get it from a pig.

bad

1. The peach is **bad.** It has a spot on it. It is not good.
2. The burglar is **bad.** He breaks the law.

badge

The policeman wears a **badge.**
A metal or cloth **badge** shows what a person does.

bag, bags

A **bag** is a paper or cloth pocket.
It opens at the top.
We carry things in **bags.**

baggage

This is **baggage.**
We carry **baggage** when we travel.

bait

The fish eats the **bait.**
Then it is caught on the hook.

bake, baking

Mother can **bake** good pies.
Baking is done in an oven.

baker, bakery

A **baker** makes bread, rolls, cookies, cake, and pie.

1. A **bakery** is the place where a **baker** works.
2. A **bakery** is a store that sells baked goods.

balance

1. The scales **balance.** The weights are equal on both sides.

2. Jenny lost her **balance.** She fell on the ice.

ball

1. A **ball** is a round plaything.

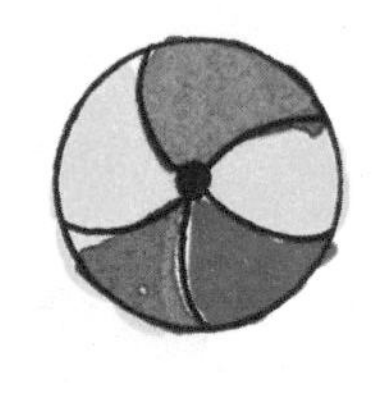

2. A **ball** is anything round. This is a **ball** of yarn.

balloon, balloons

A **balloon** is a bag of gas.

The man is selling **balloons**.

banana, bananas

A **banana** is a fruit.
Bananas grow in bunches.

band

1. Shirley has a red **band** on her hat. It is a narrow strip of cloth.

2. A **band** is a group of people. Our school **band** plays music.

bandage

Edward cut his finger.
He has a **bandage** to cover the cut.

bang

Tom closed the door with a **bang**.
He closed it with a loud noise.

bank

1. A **bank** is a place for keeping money safe. Judy has a little **bank** for her money.

2. The **bank** of the river is high. The land at the side of the river is high.

banner

The red and white **banner** is our school flag.

bar, bars

A **bar** is a long piece of metal or hard wood.
The lion cannot hurt us.
He is behind iron **bars**.

barber

The **barber** is cutting Sam's hair.

bare

Billy makes snowballs with his **bare** hands.
His hands are not covered.

barefoot

Pete is **barefoot**.
He is not wearing anything on his feet.

bargain

The apples are a **bargain**.
The price is low for such good apples.

bark

1. **Bark** is the outside skin of a tree.
2. A **bark** is a sailing ship.
3. Ralph's dog likes to **bark**.

barn

A **barn** is a farm building.
The farmer keeps hay and animals in the **barn**.

barrel

There are apples in the **barrel**.

base

1. The **base** is the lowest part of anything.
The **base** of the lamp is heavy.

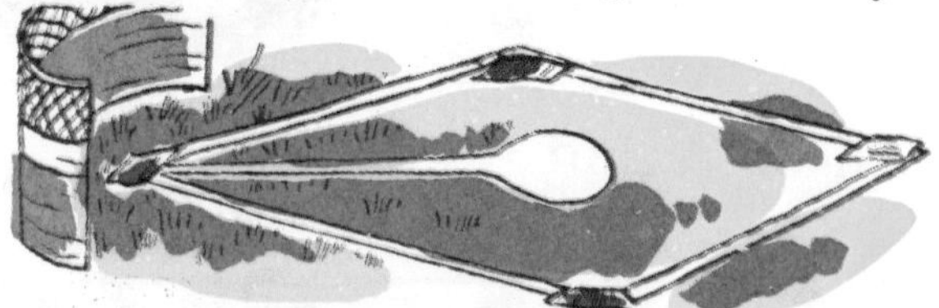

2. Each point of a baseball diamond is a **base**.

baseball

1. A **baseball** is hard.
2. **Baseball** is an American game.

beast

A **beast** is an animal.

beat, beaten

Our team tried to **beat** Joe's.
We tried to win the game.
We were **beaten**.

beautiful

We like to look at **beautiful** things.
We like to listen to **beautiful** music.
If a thing is **beautiful**, it pleases us.

because

Helen is running **because** she is late for school.
That is the reason why she runs.

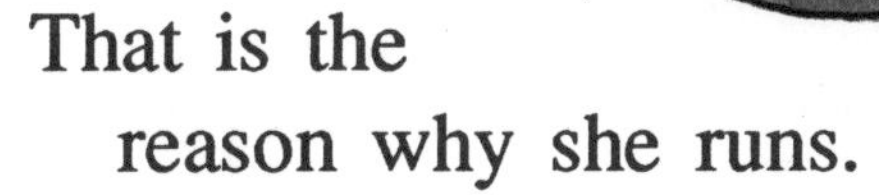

become, becoming, became

1. A seed will **become** a plant. It will grow to be a plant.
2. The hat is **becoming** to Rose.
   It looks well on Rose.
3. What **became** of the ball?
   What happened to the ball?

bed, bedroom

My **bed** is in the corner of my **bedroom**.
I sleep on my **bed**.
I sleep in the **bedroom**.

bee

The **bee** is an insect.
It makes honey and wax.

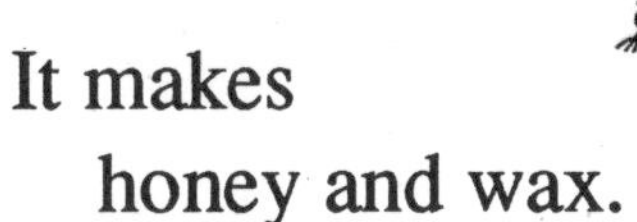

beef

Meat that we get from a cow is called **beef**.

beet

The **beet** is a vegetable.
We eat the roots and leaves.

before

1. Ten o'clock is **before** noon.
   It is earlier than noon.
2. Rose stands **before** Andrew.
   Rose stands in front of Andrew.

beg, beggar, begging

1. Topsy can **beg** for a bone.
   She asks for a bone.
2. A **beggar** lives by **begging**.

begin, beginning, began, begun

School will **begin** soon.
It will start soon.
The **beginning** of school is a happy time.
Last year school **began** early.
We have **begun** to be tired of vacation.

behave, behaved

How did Baby **behave**?
How did he act?
He **behaved** himself.
He was well **behaved**.
He was very good.

behind

John is hiding **behind** the tree.

belief

Columbus had a **belief** that the world was round.
That was what he thought.

believe, believes

I **believe** what Tom said.
Sally **believes** him, too.
We think that Tom is telling the truth.

bell

A **bell** is made of metal.
Hear the **bell** ring!

belong, belongs

These balls **belong** to Bill.
That one **belongs** to John.
John owns that ball.

below

A table is **below** the mirror.
It is lower than the mirror.

beyond

The store is **beyond** my house.
It is farther down the street.

bib

Baby wears
a **bib**
when he
eats.

It is a cloth under his chin.

bicycle

Terry rides a **bicycle.**
A **bicycle** has two wheels.

bid

I **bid** my mother good
morning.
I say good morning to her.

big, bigger, biggest

This is a **big** pear.
It is a large pear.
This one is **bigger.**
This is the **biggest.**

bill

1. The milkman has come
with the milk **bill.**
It tells what to pay.

bind, binding, bound

Philip has to **bind** the
package.
He has to tie the package.
He is **binding** it with cord.
He has **bound** it tightly.

bird, birds

A **bird** is an animal.
A **bird** has feathers.
These are **birds:**

ostrich

stork

duck

B

Block, blocks

1. There are
   five houses in my **block**.

2. These are Baby's **blocks**.

blood

Blood is a red liquid.
It runs through our bodies.

bloom

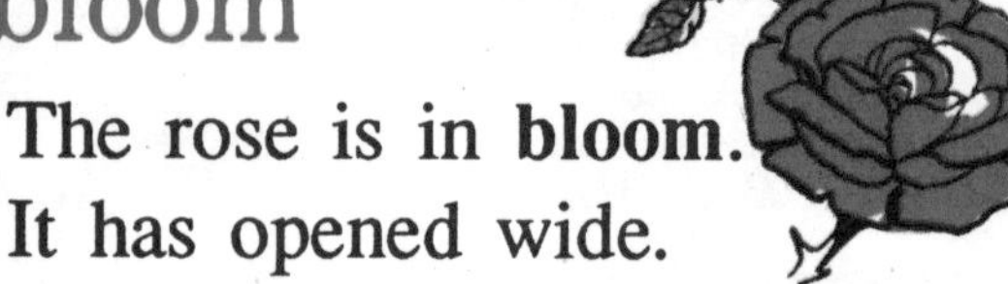

The rose is in **bloom**.
It has opened wide.

blossom, blossoms

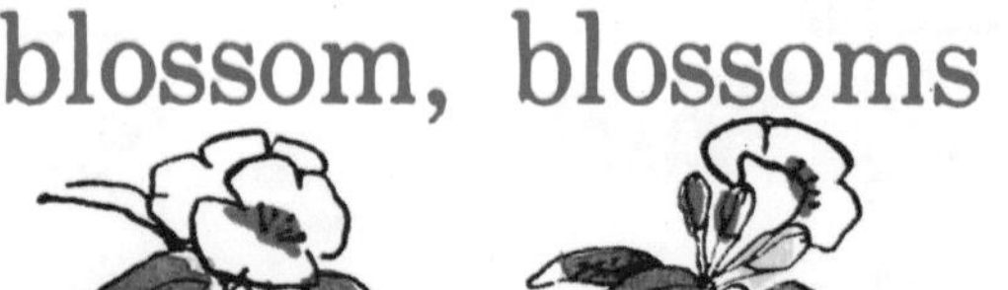

A **blossom** is a flower.
Apple **blossoms** are sweet.
Apples come from **blossoms**.

blot, blotter

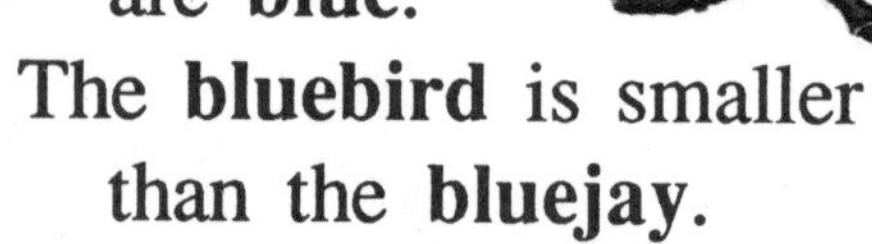

Beth will
blot the
ink.

Beth will use
a **blotter**
to dry the ink.
It is a piece of soft paper.

blouse

A **blouse** is clothing.
A **blouse** covers
the upper part of the body.
Ann has a white **blouse**.

blow, blowing, blew, blown

How hard the wind can **blow**.
It is **blowing** the washing.
It **blew** down the tree.
It has **blown** off Laura's hat.

blue, bluebird, blue jay

Blue is a
colour.
Both birds
are **blue**.
The **bluebird** is smaller
than the **bluejay**.

board

This is a **board**.
It is a piece of wood.
It is long, thin and flat.

boast

George likes to **boast**.
He is always telling how
strong he is.

boat

Edward has a red **boat**.
The **boat** floats on the water.

body, bodies

The doll's
body is
stuffed
with
cotton.
Our **bodies** have bones.

boil, boils

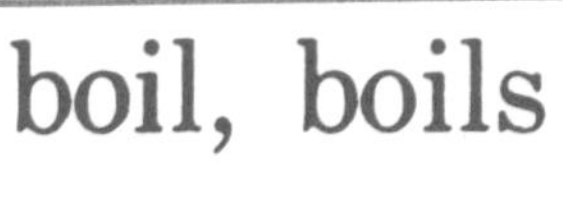

1. We **boil** water in the kettle.
When it **boils**, it bubbles.
2. Patrick has a painful
boil on his neck.

bold

The robber was **bold**.
He was not afraid.

bolt

The door is
fastened
by a **bolt**.

bone, bones

Scrappy has
a meat
bone.
These are
the **bones**
of a fish.
Bones are
the hard
parts inside
our bodies.

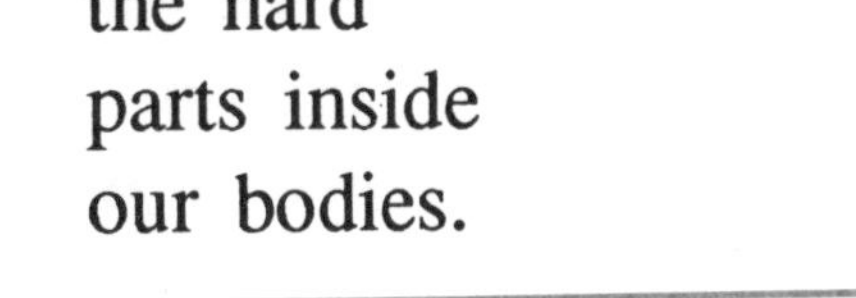

bonfire

Jim is watching a **bonfire**.
A **bonfire** is made outdoors.

bonnet

A little baby
wears a
bonnet on
its head.

book, books, bookcase

A **book** has leaves of paper.
The leaves are bound together.
We read story **books.**
We look at picture **books.**
Lena's **books** are in a **bookcase.**

bookkeeper

Mr. Fry is a **bookkeeper.**
He keeps business accounts.

boom

A **boom** is a loud noise.
A big gun makes a **boom.**

boots

Tom and Betty are wearing **boots.**
Boots cover the foot and part of the leg.

border, borders

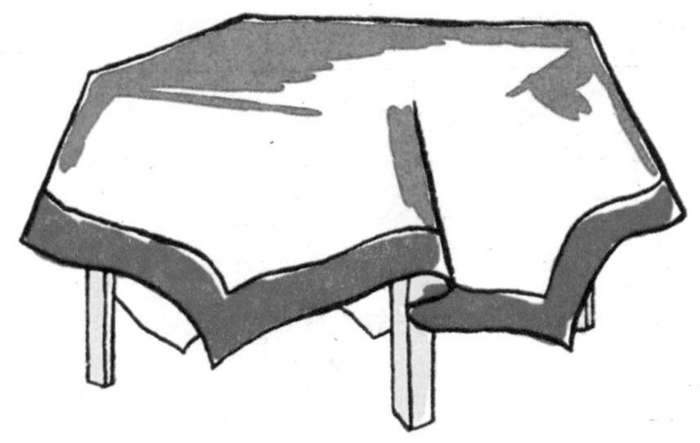

1. The tablecloth has a red **border.**

The edge of it is red.

2. Canada **borders** on the United States.

The two countries are side by side.

bore

1. Jack will **bore** a hole.
2. This story is a **bore.**
   It is not interesting.

born

Baby was **born** a year ago.
That is the time when he came into the world.

borrow

Tony asked to **borrow** my pen.
He asked to use it awhile.

both

Judy and Mary
have lollipops.
Both have lollipops.

bother

Flies cannot **bother** us.
They cannot trouble us.
Our windows have screens.

bottle

A **bottle** is used to
hold a liquid.
It has a narrow neck.

These are **bottles**.

bottom

There is a
cherry in
the **bottom**
of Jane's
glass.

The **bottom** is the lowest part
of anything.

bough

A **bough** is a
branch of a tree.

bounce

The ball can
bounce. It
jumps back when it is
thrown against something
hard.

bound, bounds

1. Ann is **bound** for school.
   She is on her way.
2. The deer **bounds** away.
   He runs with long jumps.

boundary

A fence marks
the **boundary** of our farm.
A fence marks
the edge of the farm.

bouquet

Carol Ann
has a
bouquet.
A **bouquet** is
a bunch of flowers.

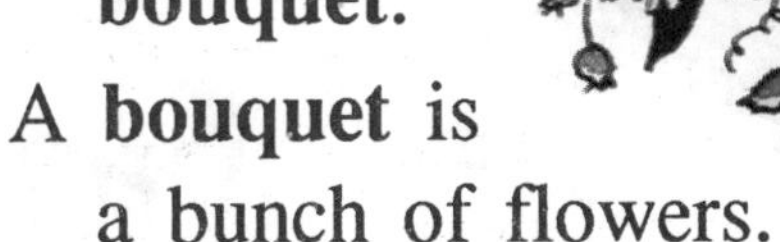

bow

1. Lena's
   sash is
   tied with
   a **bow**.
2. Ted has a
   bow and
   arrow.

bridge

A **bridge** is built to carry a roadway over the river.
People cross the river by means of the **bridge**.

brief

Philip's story is **brief**.
It is a short story.

bright, brighter, brightest

Lamplight is **bright**.
Gaslight is **brighter**.
Electric light is **brightest**.

brilliant

1. The sun is **brilliant**.
   It is very bright.
2. Martin is **brilliant**.
   He is a very good student.

brim, brimming

1. Ann's hat has a wide **brim**.
2. The cup is **brimming**.

It is full to the top.

bring, bringing, brought

Bring your ball to my house.
Come here with your ball.
John is **bringing** his bat.
He **brought** it yesterday, too.

broad

The Amazon is **broad**.
It is a wide river.

broadcast

We heard Billy **broadcast** his song.
He sang it over the radio.

broil

The boys **broil** their fish over the campfire.
They cook their fish over the campfire.

brook

We fish in the **brook**.
It is a small stream.

broom

A **broom** is used for sweeping.
Here are two kinds of **broom**.

brother

My **brother** Tom and I have the same parents.

brown

Brown is a colour.
Fred has **brown** hair.

bruise

Paul hit his knee.
He has a **bruise**.
It is black and blue.

brush, brushes

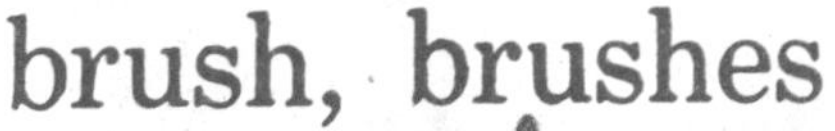

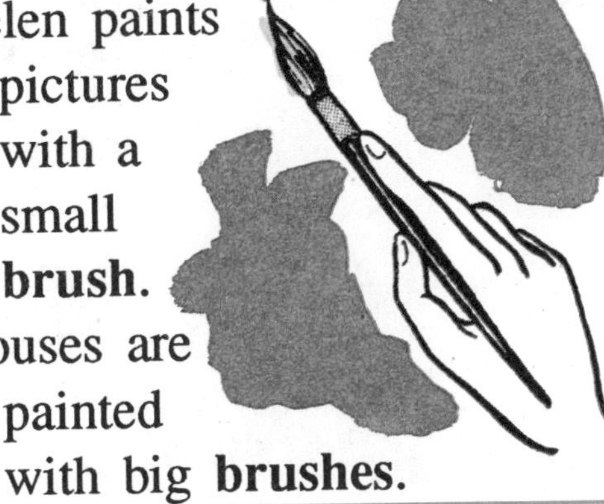

Helen paints pictures with a small **brush**.
Houses are painted with big **brushes**.

bubble

What a large **bubble** Anna is blowing!

bucket

Tom carries a **bucket** of water.
He carries a pail of water.

buckle

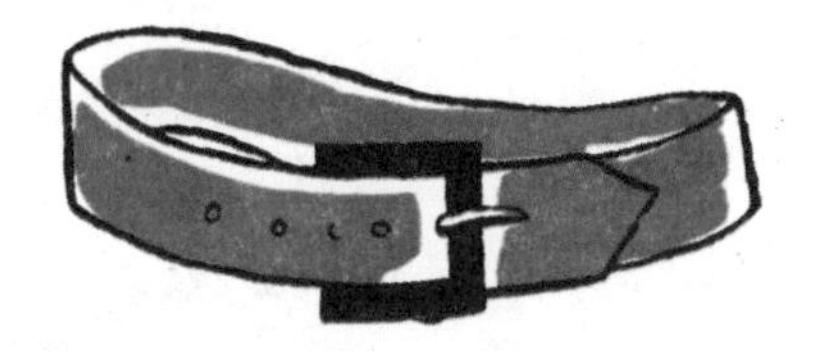

The belt is fastened with a **buckle**.

bud

This is the **bud** of a flower.
First we have the **bud**.
Then we have the flower.

buffalo, buffaloes

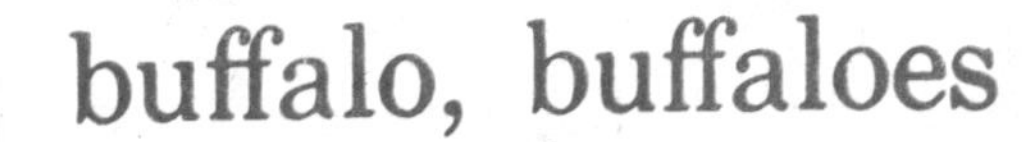

A **buffalo** is an animal of Asia.
It is like an ox.
African **buffaloes** are wild.
Bison are called **buffaloes**.

bug

A **bug** is a little insect.

busy

Mother is **busy**.
She works every minute.

but

The day is cloudy,
but there is no rain.
This surprises us.

butcher

We buy meat from the **butcher**.

butter, buttermilk

Butter is made of the fat
that is in cream.
The milk that is left
after the fat has been
taken is called **buttermilk**.

buttercup

A **buttercup**
is a yellow
flower.

butterfly, butterflies

A **butterfly** is an insect.
These are **butterflies**.

button, buttons

Mother has
to **button**
Ann's dress.
She fastens it with buttons.
These are
buttons.

buy, buying, bought

Ralph likes to **buy** sweets.
He is **buying** winegums.
He is paying for the sweets.
After he has **bought** the
winegums, he will give
some to us.

buzz

Bees **buzz**.
A **buzz** is the sound they make.

by

1. Dot waits **by** the tree. She waits beside the tree.
2. We walked **by** the mill. We walked past the mill.
3. The painting was done **by** Ann. She was the artist.

C c

cab

A **cab** is a vehicle.
It is for hire.
It carries passengers.

cabbage

A **cabbage** is a vegetable.
It is red or green.

cabin

At camp we sleep in a **cabin.**
It is a small house.

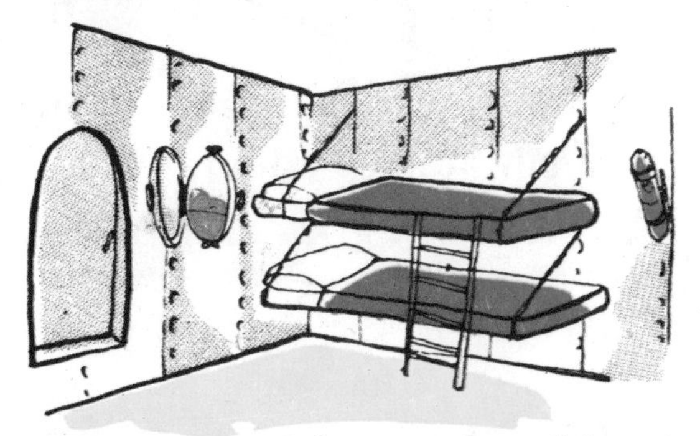

We have a **cabin** on the ship.
It is a room on the ship.

cabinet

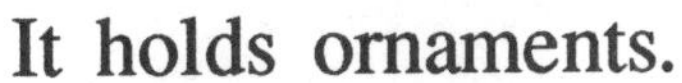

1. A **cabinet** is a cupboard.
It holds ornaments.
2. A **cabinet** is a group of people. They advise the ruler of a country.

cable, cablegram

A **cable** is a strong rope or wire.
A message sent on an undersea **cable** is called a **cablegram.**

cage

The birds are in a **cage.** It is a box with many open spaces.

cake

1. **Cake** is a food.
It is made of flour, eggs, milk, sugar, butter, and baking powder.
2. This is a **cake** of ice.

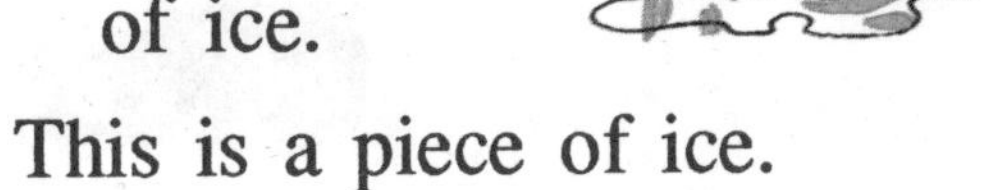

This is a piece of ice.

C D E F G H I J K L M N O P Q R S T U V W X Y Z

calendar

A **calendar**
tells
the date.

calf, calves

A **calf** is the young of a cow.
The **calves** are lively.

call

Edward is in the cornfield.
Call him to supper.
Ask him to come.
Speak in a loud voice.

calm

The day is **calm.**
It is quiet and not windy.

camel

A **camel**
is an animal with a hump.

camera

Terry's **camera**
takes good pictures.

camp, camps

John
goes to a **camp** in summer.
He has an outdoor life.
Soldiers live in **camps**.

can, canned

1. Grace **can**
skate.

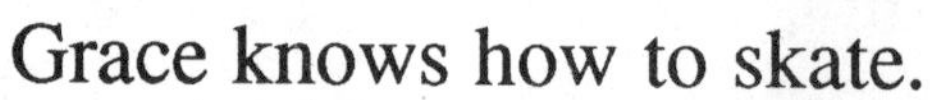

Grace knows how to skate.
2. This is a
can of fruit.
The fruit is **canned.**
It is kept for future use
in a jar of tin or glass.

canal, canalboat

Steam shovels dug the **canal.**
The **canal** is filled with water.
A **canalboat** goes on the **canal.**

canary, canaries

A **canary** is
a bird.
Canaries can sing sweetly.

candle, candlestick

A **candle** gives light.

It has a wick covered with wax.

The wick burns slowly.

The **candlestick** holds a **candle.**

candy, candies

Candy is a sweet food.

Sugar is used in **candies.**

cane

A **cane** is a stick.

Grandfather walks with the help of a **cane.**

cannon

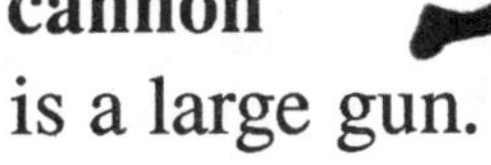

A **cannon** is a large gun.

cannot

Tom **cannot** swim.

He is not able to swim.

canoe

A **canoe** is a light boat.

canvas

Canvas is heavy cloth.

It is used for tents and sails and oil paintings.

cap

1. This pistol fires a **cap.**

A **cap** is a small package of powder.

It makes a noise when it is hit.

2. A **cap** is a covering for the head.

cape

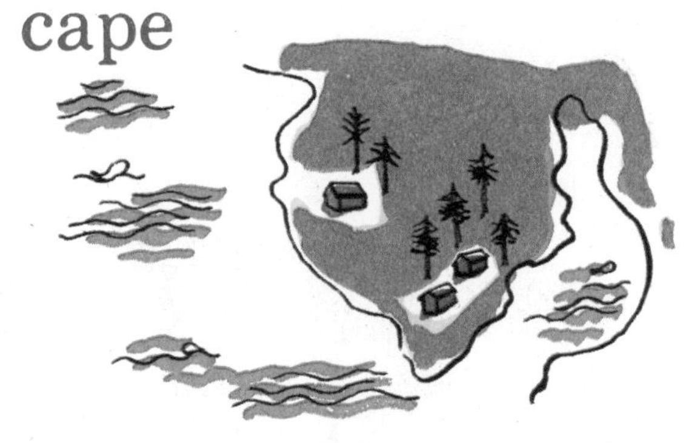

1. A **cape** is land that has water on three sides.
2. A **cape** is a full coat with no sleeves.

C D E F G H I J K L M N O P Q R S T U V W X Y Z

C D E F G H I J K L M N O P Q R S T U V W X Y Z

carpet

A **carpet** covers the floor.

carriage

A **carriage** is a vehicle.
It is pulled by horses.

carrot

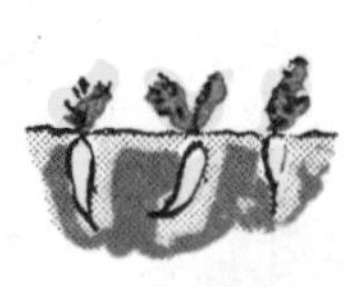

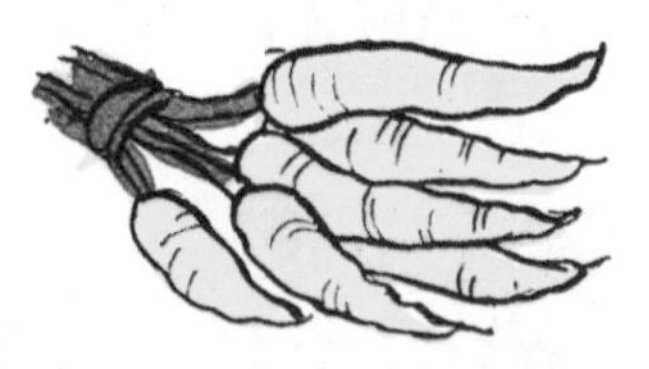

A **carrot** is a vegetable.
It grows underground.

carry, carrying, carried

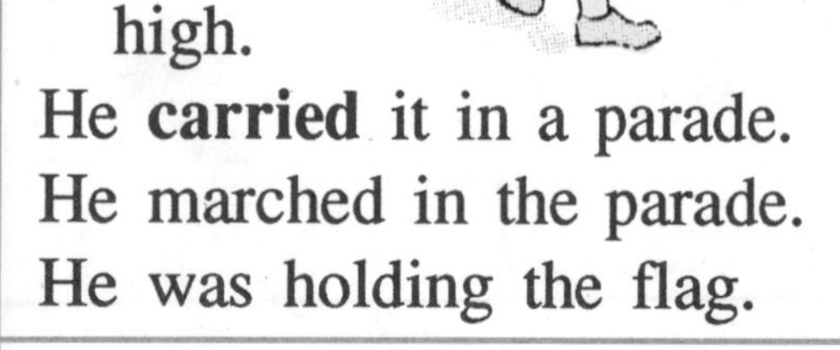

John likes to **carry** the flag.
He is **carrying** the flag high.
He **carried** it in a parade.
He marched in the parade.
He was holding the flag.

cart

A **cart** is a small vehicle.
Judy's **cart** has two wheels.

carve

Father will **carve** the meat.
He will cut slices from it.

case

A **case** is a box.
Dad is opening a **case** of canned fruit.

cash

Coins and paper money are called **cash.**

cast

1. Tony **cast** a stone.
Tony threw a stone.
2. The play had a large **cast.**
The play had many actors.

castle

The **castle** is an old
building.
It has a strong wall for
protection from enemies.

cat

A **cat** is an animal.
Sally's **cat** is a Siamese.
Paul's **cat** is a tabby.
Dora's **cat** is a Persian.

catch, catching, caught, catcher

1. Terry will **catch** some
fish.
He will get some fish.
Catching fish is fun.
He has **caught** two fish.
2. See John
catch the
ball.
He stops it
with his hand.
He is the **catcher.**

caterpillar

A **caterpillar** looks like
a fuzzy worm.
The **caterpillar** will become
a moth or a butterfly.

cattle

Cows, oxen, and the like
are animals that live
on a farm.
They are called **cattle.**

cause

The house burned down.
The **cause** of the fire
was a lighted match.
A child lighted the match.
The flame from the match
set the house on fire.

cave

A **cave** is a hollow place
in the earth or the rocks.

cease

The order came to **cease** firing.
The order came to stop firing.

cedar

A **cedar** tree is an evergreen.

ceiling

The light hangs from the **ceiling.**
The **ceiling** is the top of a room.

celebrate

We **celebrate** Armistice Day.
We have a special programme in honour of the day.

celery

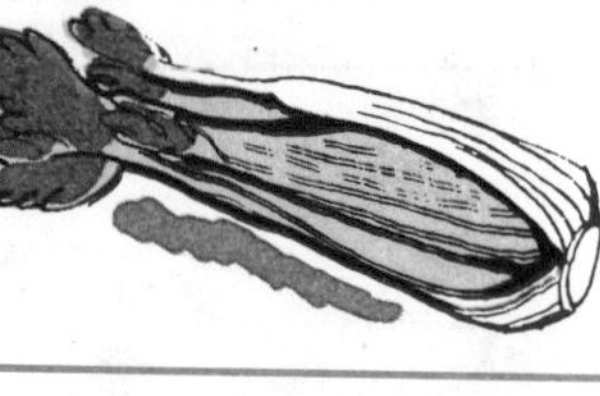

Celery is a vegetable.

cell

A **cell** is a small room.
The prisoner is in a **cell.**

cellar

A **cellar** is a room.
It is partly underground.

cement

Cement is used for building.
Cement is like stone.
Lime and clay make **cement.**

cent, cents

A **cent** is a coin.
A **cent** has little value.
100 **cents** make one dollar.

centre

Ben's arrow hit the **centre** of the target.
It hit the middle of the target.

central

The school building is in a **central** place. It is in the middle of the city.

century, centuries

A **century** is 100 years.
The earth is many **centuries** old.

cereal, cereals

1. A **cereal** is a food that is made from grain.

Oatmeal is a **cereal.**

2. **Cereals** are grains.

We eat the seeds of **cereals.**

certain

Pat is **certain** of the answer.

Pat is sure of the answer.

certainly

Helen will **certainly** come.

She will not fail to come.

chain

1. This is an iron **chain.**

It has rings of iron.

They are joined together.

2. A long line of mountains is called a mountain **chain.**

chair

A **chair** is a piece of furniture.

Helen is sitting on a **chair.**

chalk

A stick of **chalk** makes a white or coloured mark.

champion

Jerry won all the races.

Jerry is the **champion.**

chance

Bingo is a game of **chance.**

The game is won by luck.

change

1. Lois will **change** her dress

She will take off one dress and put on another dress.

2. Grace spent 95 pence.

She gave the man a pound.

He gave her 5 pence **change.**

channel

A **channel** is a path in which a liquid runs.

The river has a deep **channel.**

chapter

Helen read a **chapter.**

A **chapter** is a part of a book. There are several pages in a **chapter.**

C D E F G H I J K L M N O P Q R S T U V W X Y Z

character

1. Annie has a kind **character.**

She is a kind person.

2. A **character** is a person in a book or play.

charge

1. A man repaired our radio.

He made a **charge** of £5.00.

He set a price of £5.00 for putting our radio in order.

2. Dick takes **charge** of the books.

charm, charms

1. Rose has **charm.**

She is lovely.

2. The Fairy said a **charm.**

She said magic words, and the frog became a prince.

3. Dot has three **charms** on her bracelet.

chase

Toby likes to **chase** birds.

He runs after them.

He tries to catch them.

chatter

The children **chatter.**

They talk fast.

cheap, cheaper, cheapest

The first hat is **cheap.**

The price of the hat is low.

The second hat is **cheaper.**

The third hat is **cheapest.**

cheat

Dad says, "Never **cheat.** Always be honest in work or in play."

check, checks

1. Uncle John **checks** into the hotel.

This is to register his arrival.

2. Pat's shirt has a pattern of **checks.**

It has a pattern of squares.

checkers

Checkers is a game.

We are playing **checkers.**

choose, choosing, chose, chosen

Jane must **choose** a partner.
She must pick a partner.
Choosing is hard for her.
Jane **chose** Jonathan.
I should have **chosen** Dick.

chop

1 Ruth ate a lamb **chop.**
A **chop** is a small piece of meat.

2. Harry will **chop** down the tree.
He will cut it down by cutting chips from it with an axe.

chorus

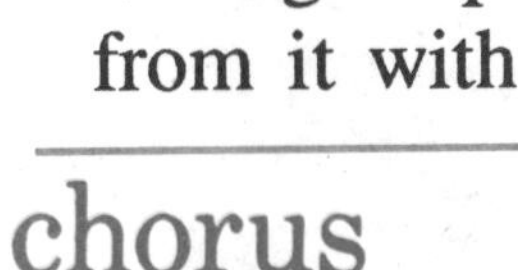

1. A **chorus** is a group of singers or speakers.
Ann belongs to a **chorus.**
2. They sang a **chorus.**
They sang a song.
3. We were asked to join in singing the **chorus.**
We were asked to sing the last part of the song.

church, churches

A **church** is a building.
We worship God in **churches.**

cigar, cigarette

A **cigar** is a roll of tobacco.
A **cigarette** is made of tobacco, cut fine and rolled in paper.

circle

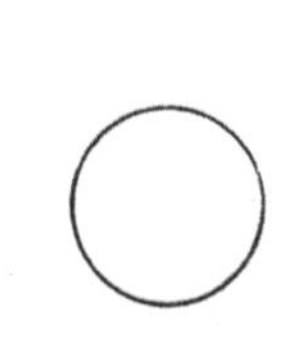

A **circle** is round.
We stand in a **circle.**

circus, circuses

Have you seen the **circus**?
A **circus** is an entertainment.
Circuses have trained animals, music, acrobats, and clowns.

citizen, citizens

Dad is a **citizen** of this country. He was born here.

Pat's father came from Italy.

He chose to become a **citizen** of this country.

A country protects the lives and property of **citizens.**

It is the duty of a **citizen** to obey the laws of his country.

city, cities

A **city** is a community.

Many people live together in a **city.**

Some **cities** are governed by a mayor and council.

claim, claimed

1. Beth's dog was lost.

The dog has been found.

She will go to **claim** it.

She will ask to have her dog.

2. Several countries **claimed** land in North America.

Several countries said they had a right to the land.

clam

A **clam** has a hard shell.

We eat the fish that is in the shell.

clap

In this dance we **clap** our hands.

We hit our hands together.

class

A **class** is a group of pupils who are taught together.

claw

Pussy has a **claw** on each toe.

It is a sharp nail.

clay

Clay is sticky earth.

We are making **clay** dishes.

clean, cleaner

Jack washed his hands.

He thinks that they are **clean.**

They could be **cleaner.**

coarse
The cloth is **coarse.**
It is rough.

coast
The **coast** is land on the
edge of the sea.

coat

A **coat** is
clothing.
Joan wears
a blue **coat.**

coax
Coax Jane to come with us.
Ask her in a pleasant way.

cocoa
Cocoa is a drink made from
milk and powdered cacao.

coconut

The **coconut**
is a large
nut with a
thick shell.

cocoon

The caterpillar
has spun a **cocoon.**
It is inside the **cocoon.**

coffee, coffeepot

Coffee is a drink made
from the seeds of berries.
It is made in a **coffeepot.**

coin

A **coin** is metal money.

cold, colder, coldest
1. Joe has a **cold.**
He sneezes and feels sick.
2. The weather is **cold.**
It makes us shiver.
Monday was **colder** than
today.
It was the **coldest** day
that we have had in years.

collar

Spot wears a **collar**
around his neck.

Jane's
collar is
white.

collect, collection
1. Jim likes to **collect**
different kinds of stamps.
He gathers them and
saves them in a book.
He has a large **collection.**
2. A **collection** was taken
at the meeting. People
were asked to give
money.

C D E F G H I J K L M N O P Q R S T U V W X Y Z

college

After Bob leaves high school, he will go to **college.**
College is a higher school.

collie

Prince is Dot's dog.
He is a **collie.**

colonel

A **colonel** is an officer in the army.

colour, colours, coloured

Red is a **colour.**
Orange is a **colour.**
Yellow is a **colour.**
Green is a **colour.**
Blue is a **colour.**
The picture is printed in **colours.**
It is **coloured.**

colt

A **colt** is an animal.
A **colt** is a young horse.

column

1. A **column** is part of a building.
It supports the roof.
2. This is a **column** of figures.

4
3
7
2
6

comb

My **comb** is blue.
A **comb** has teeth.
It is used for smoothing hair.

come, coming, came, come

Come play in my yard.
Be here early.
Carol is **coming** soon.
My new swing **came** today.
Jane has **come** already.

comet

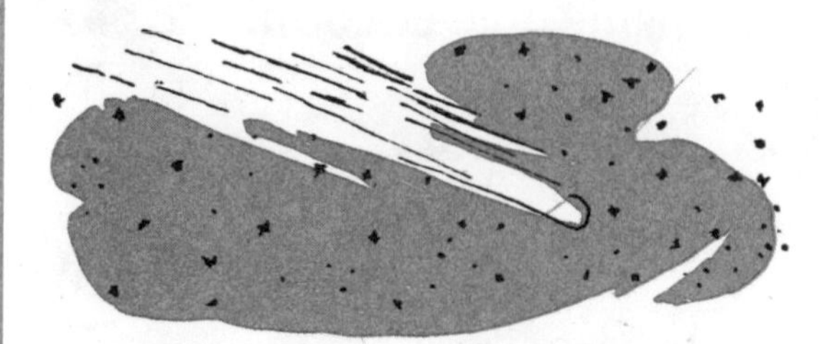

A **comet** looks like a star with a tail of light.

concern

Jane's question does not **concern** our lesson.
It has nothing to do with our lesson.

concert

Pieces of music are sung or played at a **concert**.

condition

1. The car is in **condition** for use.
It is in a state for use.
It is ready for use.

2. We shall have the picnic on Saturday, on the **condition** that we have good weather.
If we have good weather, we shall have the picnic.

conduct, conducts

Harry's **conduct** is good.
He **conducts** himself well.
He behaves well.

conductor

A **conductor** is a person in charge of a public vehicle.
The **conductor** collects fares.

cone

A **cone** has this shape.

Alice has an ice cream **cone**.

confess

Carol Ann will **confess** that she did wrong.
She will say that she did wrong to break the vase.

congress

Congress is a group of people elected by the citizens.
They meet to make laws.

connect, connection

Ted will **connect** two ropes.
He will join the ends of the ropes.
The **connection** will be made by means of a knot.

C D E F G H I J K L M N O P Q R S T U V W X Y Z

conquer

The king tried to **conquer** the nearby countries.
He tried to bring them under his rule by force.

conscience

Conscience tells us what is right and what is wrong.

consent

Ask Tom to help us.
He will **consent** to help us.
He will be willing to help us.

consider

We must **consider** the rights of others.
We must give thought to the rights of others.

constitution

A **constitution** is a set of laws for a group of people.

consult

Mother will **consult** the doctor.
She will ask his advice.

contain

What does the box **contain**?
What is in the box?

content

Susy is **content** with her toys.
She wishes nothing more.

contest

We had a spelling **contest**.
Bessie won the **contest**.
She spelled more words right than the others did.

continent, continents

A **continent** is a large area of land.

There are seven **continents**:

Africa	South America
Asia	Australia
Europe	Antarctica
North America	

continue

After a fire drill, we **continue** our work.
We go on with our work.

cotton

Cotton grows on a **cotton** plant.
Cloth is made from **cotton.**

couch

A **couch** is a piece of furniture.
People sit on a **couch.**
Dad takes a nap on the **couch.**

cough

Russell has a chest cold.
He has a bad **cough.**

could

May knew that she **could** do it.
She knew that she was able to do it.

council

A **council** is a group of people who give advice to the leaders.

count

Count the puppies.
One, two, three, four.
I **count** four puppies.

counter

Peggy is at the **counter.**
It is a long table.

country, countries

1. We go to the **country** in summer. We see much land and not many houses.
2. A **country** is the land that belongs to a nation.

Brazil is a **country**.
There are many **countries** in South America.

county, counties

A **county** is larger than a city.
Countries or states may be divided into **counties.**

crooked

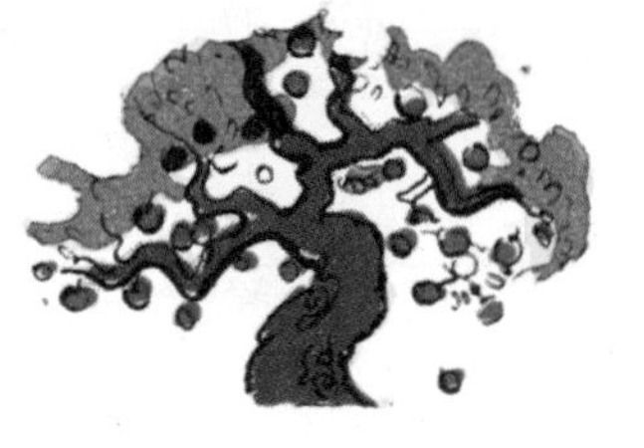

The old
tree is
crooked.
It is not straight.

crop

We have
picked all the apples.
We have a fine apple **crop**.

cross, crossing

1. There is a
cross on
the top of the steeple.

2. We **cross** the brook.
We go over to the other
side.
We are **crossing** on a bridge.
3. Father is **cross**. He is
angry.

crow

The **crow** is
a bird. It is black.

crowd

A **crowd** is on the beach.
Many people are on the
beach.

crown

The king
wears a gold
crown on his head.

cruel

The king was **cruel**.
He was unkind.

crumb

The bird has a bread **crumb**.
It has a bit of bread.

crush

Do not step on the flowers.
You will **crush** them.
You will destroy them.

crust

Ann ate the soft part
of the bread, but not
the **crust**.

crutch

Ted broke his leg.
He uses a **crutch** for aid in walking.

cry, crying, cried

Let Baby **cry**.
Let him make a noise.
Soon he will stop **crying**.
He **cried** because he was angry.

cube

This is a **cube**.

cucumber

A **cucumber** is a vegetable.
It is long and green.

cuff

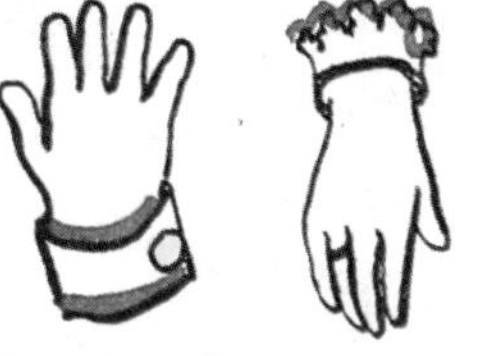

A **cuff** is part of a sleeve.
It is the part at the wrist.

cultivate

Farmers **cultivate** soil.
They work the soil so that it will grow crops.

cunning

The fox is **cunning**.
He is clever at tricks.

cup

A **cup** is a dish.
This is a tea **cup**.

cupboard

Food and dishes are kept in a **cupboard**. Mother Hubbard's **cupboard** was bare.

cure

Ann is sick in bed.
The doctor will **cure** her.
He will make her well.

curl, curly

Virginia has a **curl** on her forehead.
Her hair is **curly**.
It is not straight.

currant

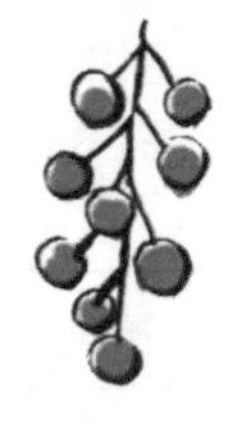

The **currant** is a small fruit.

current

A **current** is moving water. The river has a rapid **current**.

curtain, curtains

The theatre **curtain** is wide. We have **curtains** at the window.

curve, curved

A **curve** is a line which is not straight in any part. The road is **curved**.

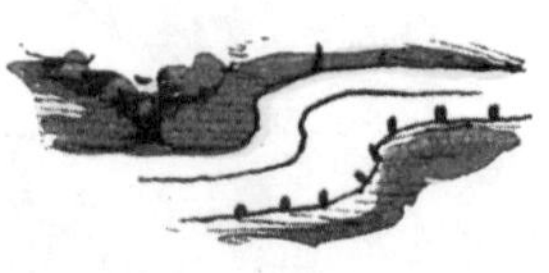

cushion

Inkie sleeps on a **cushion**. It is a bag stuffed with something soft.

custard

Custard is a food made of eggs and milk.

custom

It is Grandma's **custom** to take a nap after dinner. She usually sleeps then.

customer

A **customer** is one who buys. The **customer** is buying meat.

cut

The cake has been **cut** with a knife.

cylinder

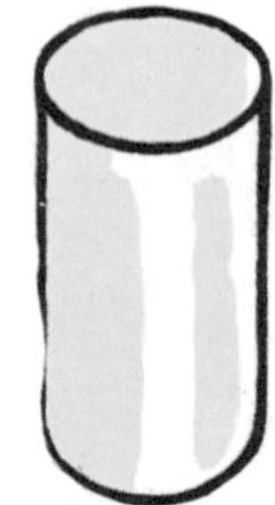

1. A **cylinder** has this shape.
2. A **cylinder** is part of an automobile engine.

C D E F G H I J K L M N O P Q R S T U V W X Y Z

D d

dad, daddy

Dad is a name for father.
Often we call him **Daddy**.

daffodil

A **daffodil** is a yellow flower.

daily

We take a **daily** paper.
It comes every day.

dainty

The fairy is **dainty**.

She is small and graceful.

dairy

1. On a farm, a **dairy** is a place where milk is kept and made into butter or cheese.
2. A **dairy** is a store in which milk, cream, butter and eggs are sold.

daisy, daisies

A **daisy** is a flower. Its petals grow around a centre.
Jane picked some **daisies** in a sunny field.

dam

The **dam** is built across the river.
It holds back the water.

damage

The car ran into a wall.
Damage was done to the bumper bar.
The bumper bar was badly bent.

dear

1. Ann is my **dear** sister.
I am very fond of her.
2. The coat is **dear**.
It has a high price.

death

The king ruled until his **death**.
He ruled to the end of his life.

debt

I owe Tom five pence.
That is a **debt**.

deceive

The scarecrow is put in the field to **deceive** the crows.
It gives them a false idea.
They think it is a man.

decide, decision

Laura cannot **decide** which doll is best. She is not able to make a **decision**.
She cannot make up her mind.

deck

1. We are on the ship's **deck**.
The **deck** is a wooden floor built over part of the ship.
2. A **deck** of cards is a pack of cards.

3. We **deck** the hall with holly.
We trim the hall with holly.

declare

Pat and Martin **declare** that they are tired.
They say that they are tired.

decorate, decoration

We all help to **decorate** the tree.
We trim it. The **decoration** on the top is a star.

deed

1. We have a **deed**.
The **deed** says in writing that we own our house.
2. The boy did a brave **deed**.
He did a brave act.

deep, deeper, deepest

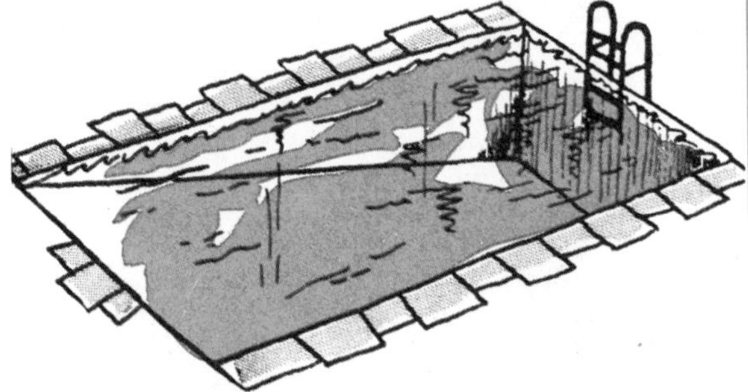

The pool is **deep**. The bottom is far below the top.
It is **deeper** at one end.
It is **deepest** by the ladder.

deer

A **deer** is an animal.
We saw two **deer**.

defeat

Dad can **defeat** me in games.
I cannot win when he plays.

defend, defence

Soldiers **defend** their country.
They fight in **defence** of their country.
They try to keep their country from danger.

degree, degrees

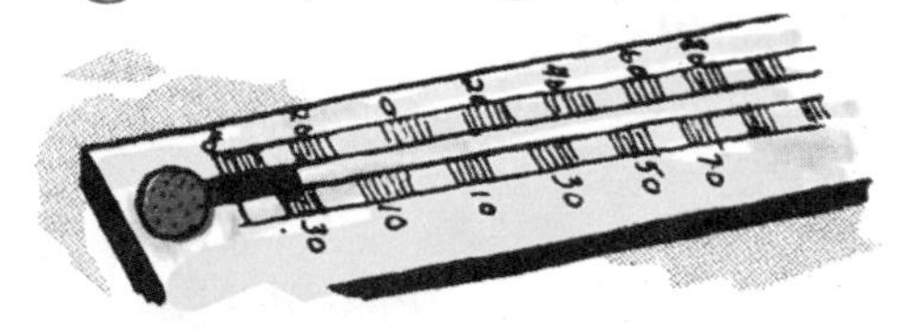

A **degree** is one step.
A thermometer marks the **degrees** of heat or cold.

delay

The children will not go to bed.
They **delay** going to bed.
They are slow about going.

delicate

A spider's web is **delicate**.
It is light and thin.

delicious

Ice cream is **delicious**.
It tastes good.

D E F G H I J K L M N O P Q R S T U V W X Y Z

destroy

The men will **destroy** the
old building.
They will tear down the
old building.

dew

Dew is formed at night
on the cool grass.
In the morning the grass
has drops of water on it.

dial

1. The face
of a watch
or clock is
called a
dial.

2. This is a
telephone
dial.

diamond

A **diamond** is a jewel.
Gloria has a **diamond** ring.

dictionary, dictionaries

A **dictionary** is a book of
words from A to Z.
This book is a **dictionary**.
Dictionaries give the
meanings of words.

die

Ann waters
her plant
every day.
If she forgot
the plant would **die.**

different, difference

One rabbit is **different**
from the other rabbits.
One rabbit is black.
The others are white.
The **difference** is in colour.

difficult

This trick is **difficult.**
It is hard to do.

dig, digging, dug

Rover will **dig** a hole.
He is **digging** in the yard.
He has **dug** a deep hole.

dim

The light is **dim.**
It is not bright.

dog, dogs

A **dog** is an animal.
Dogs are kept as pets.
Prince is a big **dog**.
Fluffy is a little **dog**.

doll

A **doll** is a toy.
This **doll** looks just like a little girl.

dollar

A **dollar** is money.
It is worth one hundred pence.
A paper **dollar** is green.
A silver **dollar** is heavy.

donkey

A **donkey** is an animal.
It is used to carry loads.
The **donkey** has long ears.

door

A **door** is part of a house.
It covers an opening.
Mother opened the front **door**.

dot, dots

A **dot** is a small circle.
There are red **dots** on Lena's dress.

double

1. This is a **double** house.
It has two parts just alike.

2. Philip's cake is **double** the size of mine.
It is twice the size of mine.

3. This is a single rose.
This is a **double** rose.
The **double** rose has more petals.

doubt, doubtful

I **doubt** Tom's story.
I am **doubtful** of the story.
I am not sure that it is true.

dough

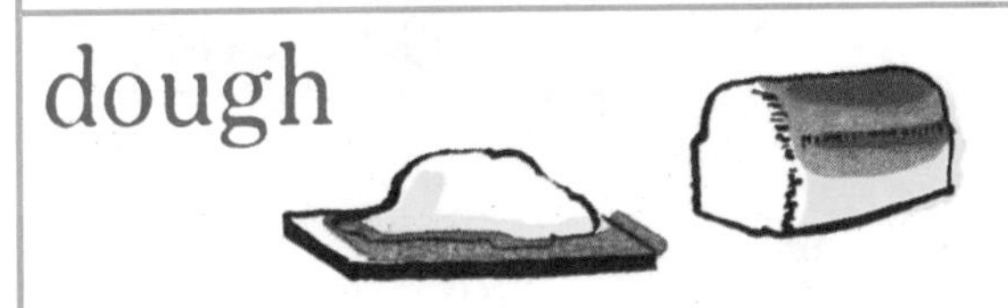

Dough is made of flour and other materials.
The **dough** rises.
Then it is made into loaves.
The loaves are baked.
The **dough** becomes bread.

doughnut

A **doughnut** is a fried cake.

dove

This bird is a **dove**.
It is a small pigeon.

down

1. We coast **down** the hill.
We coast from the top to the bottom of the hill.
2. The quilt is stuffed with **down**. It is stuffed with soft feathers.

downstairs

Annie goes **downstairs** to the cellar.

downtown

Mother took Ann **downtown**.
They went to the shops.

dozen

Twelve things make a **dozen**.

drag

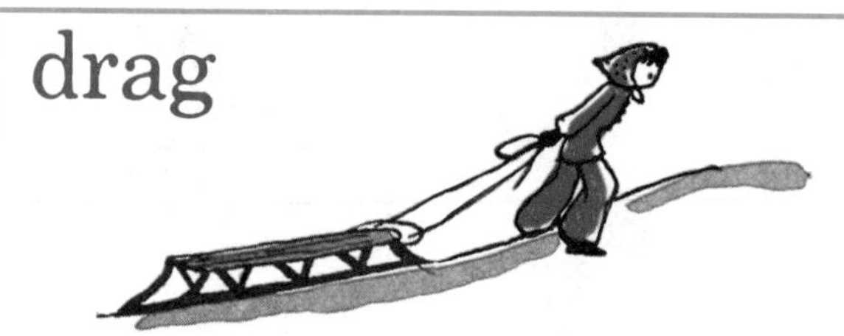

We have to **drag** our sleds up the hill.
We pull them up the hill.

dragon, dragons

A **dragon** is an imaginary beast.
We read about **dragons** in old stories.

drain

Water runs out of the sink or tub through the **drain**.

draw, drawing, drew, drawn

Joyce likes to **draw**.
She is **drawing** a lady.
She **drew** a house.
She has **drawn** the pictures with coloured chalk.

drum

A **drum** is an instrument for making sound. Roy beats his **drum** with sticks.

dry, drying, dried

After washing ourselves we **dry** our skins with a towel. We wipe off the water.
Ann is **drying** her hands.
She has **dried** her face.

duck, duckling

The **duck** is a fowl.
The **duck** has webbed feet.
They help her to swim.
She teaches her **duckling.**
She teaches the young **duck**.

due

The magazine is **due** today.
It should come today.

dull

The knife is **dull.**
It is not sharp.

dumb

The Teddy bear is **dumb**. He cannot speak.

dump

The men **dump** the ashes into the big truck.

during

Dad slept **during** the storm.
He slept while it was going on.

dust, dusty

Dot is sweeping the rug.
The rug is full of **dust**.
It is **dusty**.
It is full of fine dirt.

duty

A **duty** is an action which one ought to do.
Feeding the cat is Ann's **duty**.
She has been given that task to do.

dwarf

A **dwarf** is a tiny person.

dwell

We **dwell** in a large house.
We live in a large house.

dye

The pink curtain is faded.
We can **dye** it red.
We can soak it in **dye** to change the colour.

dynamite

Dynamite is a material which will explode. The men broke the big rock with **dynamite**.
They blew the rock to pieces.

Ee

each

Mandy, Joan, Sally, and Helen are wearing hair ribbons.
Each girl has a hair ribbon.

eager

Ann is **eager** to go to school.
She would like to go.

eagle

The **eagle** is a large bird.
It has sharp claws.

ear, ears

1. An **ear** is part of the body.
We hear with our **ears**.
Animals have **ears**.
2. An **ear** is the head of a grain plant.
This is an **ear** of corn.
This is an **ear** of oats.

early, earlier, earliest

Ann awoke at seven o'clock.
She awoke **early** in the morning.
Tom awoke an hour **earlier**.
Mother awoke **earliest**.
She was awake at five o'clock.

education

Everything we learn is part of our **education**.
It is part of our training.

effect

Peter weeds his garden.
The **effect** is a neat garden.
Because he pulls the weeds, Peter has a neat garden.

effort

Joan must make an **effort** to do well in arithmetic.
She must try hard.

egg, eggs

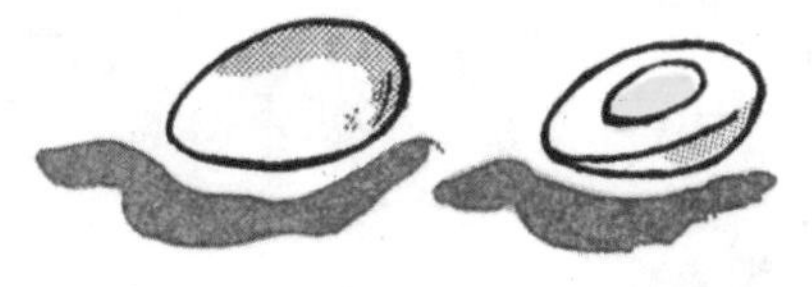

An **egg** has a shell. Inside are white and yellow parts.
Birds, snakes, fish and other animals lay **eggs**.
We eat hen's **eggs**.

eight

We have **eight** fingers and two thumbs.
4 and 4 are 8.
4 times 2 are 8.

eighteen

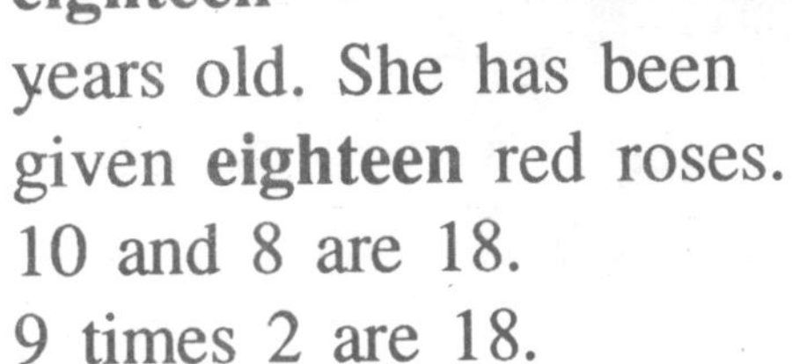

Anna is **eighteen** years old. She has been given **eighteen** red roses.
10 and 8 are 18.
9 times 2 are 18.

eighth

Tom is in the **eighth** grade.
He has been in school for **eight** years.

eighty

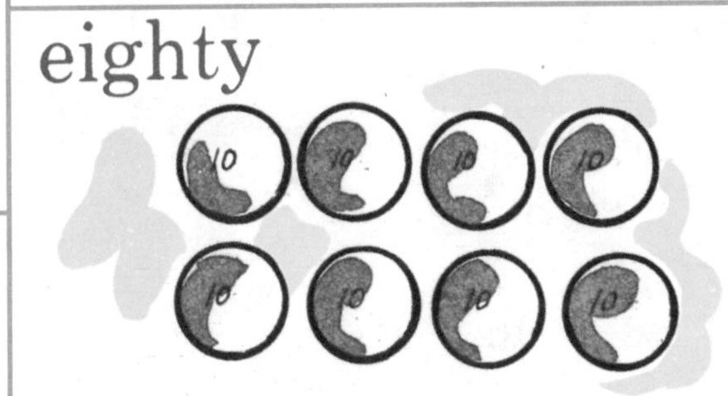

Laura has eighty pence.
She has **eighty** pence.
10 times 8 are 80.

either

Either Ann or I must go to the store for mother.
One of us must go.

elastic

Rubber is **elastic**.
It stretches and snaps back.

elbow

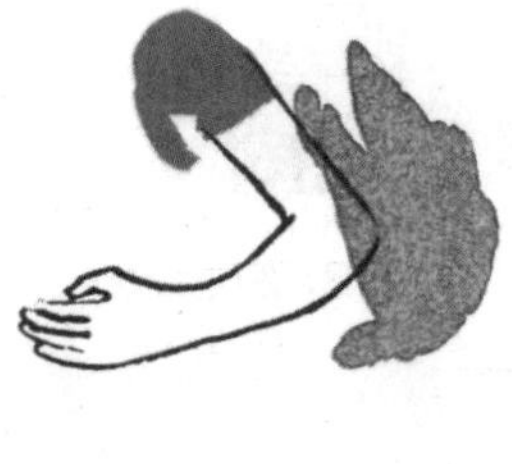

An **elbow** is a joint.
We bend the arm at the **elbow**.

E F G H I J K L M N O P Q R S T U V W X Y Z

enjoy

I **enjoy** parties. I have a good time at parties.

enormous

The factory is **enormous**.
It is very large.

enough

We have **enough** to eat.
We have all that we need.

ensign

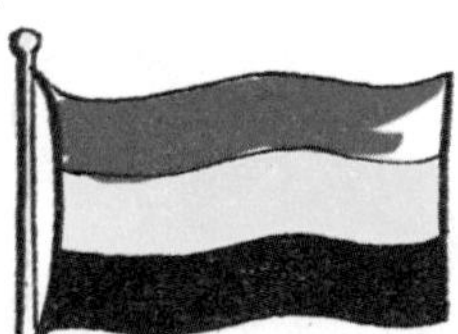

1. An **ensign** is a flag.
2. An **ensign** is an officer in the navy.

enter

Spot asked to **enter**.
He asked to come in.

entertain

Edwin likes to **entertain** us.
He likes to amuse us.

entertainment

We gave an **entertainment**.
We gave a programme for people to enjoy.

entire

I could eat an **entire** melon.
I could eat a whole melon.

entitle, entitled

1. The tickets **entitle** us to seats in the balcony.
The tickets give us the right to seats in the balcony.
2. The book is **entitled** "Heidi." That is its name.

entrance

This is the park **entrance**.
We go into the park here.

envelope

An **envelope** is a paper cover for a letter or papers.

equal

Mother used **equal** amounts of nuts and raisins.
She used one cup of nuts.
She used one cup of raisins.

erase

I shall **erase** the answer.
I shall rub it out.

eraser

A pencil **eraser** is made of rubber.
It erases pencil marks.
A blackboard **eraser** is made of cloth.
It erases chalk marks.

erect

1. Toby sits **erect**.
He sits up straight.
2. The workmen will **erect** a building here.
They will put up a building.

errand

Sam has an **errand** to do.
He must go to the store to get some bread.

error

Ann says the earth is flat.
Ann's idea is an **error**.
Her idea is wrong.

escape

The tiger cannot **escape**.
He cannot get free.

estate

Mr. Post sells real **estate**.
He sells houses and land.

even

1. The **even** numbers can be exactly divided by two.
2 4 6 8 are **even** numbers.

2. The ribbons are of **even** length.
They are the same length.
3. Baby likes vegetables.
He **even** likes spinach.
This surprises Ann.

evening

Evening is the time of night between sunset and bedtime.

event

The race was the last **event** at the picnic.
It was the last thing to happen.

exhibit, exhibition

We shall **exhibit** our
drawings.
We shall have an **exhibition**.
We shall put the drawings
up for visitors to see.

exist

No people **exist** on the moon.
No people live there.

exit

The **exit** is
the way
to go out.

expect

When the clouds look
dark, we **expect** rain.
We think that it will rain.

expense, expensive

Dad says a dog is an **expense**.
It costs money to feed a dog.
A fur
jacket is
expensive.
It costs many pounds.

expert

Mother is an **expert** cook.
She knows how to cook well.

explain

I do not know this word.
The dictionary will **explain** it.
The dictionary will tell
what the word means.

explode

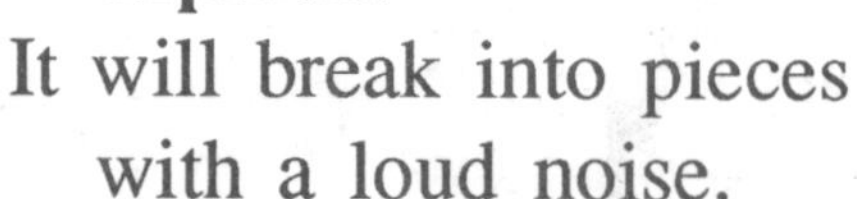

The firecracker will
explode.
It will break into pieces
with a loud noise.

explore, explorers

Men went to **explore** the desert.
They went to a strange land.
They found out what it
was like.
They were **explorers**.

export

We **export** food. We send
food to other countries.

express

1. Sam tried to **express** his idea. He tried to tell it so that we would understand it.
2. We sent the trunk by **express**.

An **express** company moves baggage, packages and other things.

3. An **express** train is a fast train making few stops.

extend

1. We **extend** our hands.

We hold out our hands.

2. Mother plans to **extend** the flower bed. She plans to make it longer.

extra

I have two umbrellas.
I need only one.
You may borrow the **extra** umbrella.

extreme

Extreme heat is needed to bake our clay dishes.
The highest degree of heat is needed.

eye, eyes

1. An **eye** is part of the body.

We see with our **eyes**.

2. The needle has an **eye**.

The thread goes through the **eye**.

3. The potato has **eyes**.

The **eyes** are seeds of potato plants.

eyebrow

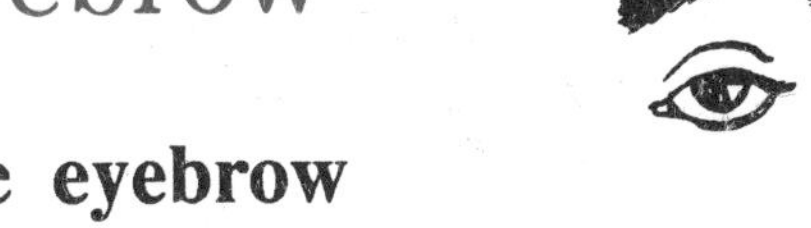

The **eyebrow** is a line of hair.
It grows above the eye.

eyeglasses

Eyeglasses are worn by people who do not see well.
Eyeglasses improve their sight.

eyelash, eyelashes

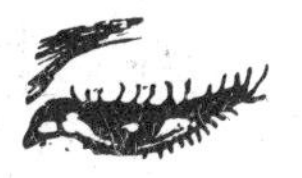

An **eyelash** is a hair. It grows on the edge of the eyelid.
Eyelashes protect the eye.

eyelid, eyelids

An **eyelid** is a fold of skin.
Eyelids cover our eyes.

F
G
H
I
J
K
L
M
N
O
P
Q
R
S
T
U
V
W
X
Y
Z

F f

fable

Mother told us a **fable** about
the hare and the tortoise.
It was a short story. It
taught us that slow,
steady people often win.

face, faces

1. The **face** is the
front part of the head.
We have happy **faces**.
2. The **face** of the
clock is the part
on which numbers are
marked.

3. We **face** the flag
when we salute it.
We turn towards the flag.

fact

Our school has 600 pupils.
This is a statement of a **fact**.
This is a true statement.

factory, factories

A **factory** is a building
in which goods are made.
This **factory** makes aeroplanes.
Many other things
are made in **factories**.

fade

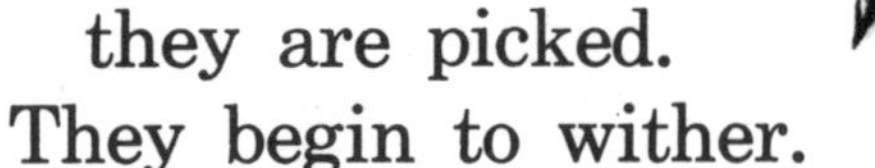

1. Flowers **fade** when
they are picked.
They begin to wither.
2. Washing made my dress
fade.
The colour became lighter.

fail, failure

The boys
try to hit the ball.
When they **fail** to hit the
ball, the team loses a point.
When they do not hit the
ball, the team loses a point.
Failure means not to do
what one is trying to do.

faint

Jayne feels **faint**.
She feels weak and dizzy.

fair, fairer, fairest

1. The queen was **fair**.
She was very pretty.
Snow White was **fairer**.
The queen thought herself
the **fairest** in the land.

2. The weather is **fair**.
The weather is good.

3. We went to a **fair**.
We bought some goods.
We saw many things
that amused us.

4. The decision is **fair**.
The decision is right.

5. Jennie has **fair** hair.
Jennie has light hair.

fairy, fairies

The **fairy** waved her wand.
The pumpkin became a coach.
Fairies are imaginary people.
They have magic power.

faith

The plane was damaged.
The pilot had **faith** in God.
He believed that God
would help him get back
to the airfield.

faithful

Prince is a
faithful watch dog.
He is watching Baby.
Prince can be trusted not
to go away from his post.

fall, falling, fell, fallen

Leaves **fall** from the tree.
They come down from the
tree.
They are **falling** fast.
Some **fell** into the pond.
Some have **fallen** on the path

false

The news was **false**.
The news was not true.

false face

Ray is wearing
a **false face.**
He is wearing a mask.

falsehood

Ben told a **falsehood**.
What he said was not true.

familiar

This street is **familiar**.
I have always lived here.
I know it well.

family

Our whole **family** had a ride.
Mother, Dad, and the children all had a ride.

famine

The country had a **famine**.
There was little food for the people to eat.

famous

The general is **famous**.
His name and deeds are known all over the world.

fan

A **fan** is something used to stir the air and cool us.

fancy, fancies

1. Rose has a **fancy** for this hat.
She has a wish for the hat.
2. The hat is **fancy**.
It has much trimming.
3. Paul has some odd **fancies**.
He has some odd ideas.

far, farther, farthest

1. Brazil is **far** from us.
It is many miles away.
Argentina is **farther** away.
The South Pole is **farthest** away.
2. Rose is **far** older than I.
Rose is much older than I.

fare

1. A **fare** is the price paid for a ride in a public vehicle.

2. The taxicab has one **fare**.
The taxicab has one passenger.

farewell

We gave Rose a **farewell** party.
She was going on a trip.
Her friends said goodbye.

F G H I J K L M N O P Q R S T U V W X Y Z

farm, farmer

A **farm** is land used
to raise crops or animals.
On Uncle Henry's **farm** we see
hay, corn, and vegetables.
He has a pasture for cows.
He has fine apple trees.
Uncle Henry owns the **farm**.
He is a **farmer**.

fashion

Once it was
the **fashion**
for girls to dress like this.
Today it is
the **fashion**
for girls to dress like this.
Fashion is the way
most people dress or act.

fast, faster, fastest

Dick can run **fast**.
He can run quickly.
Edward runs **faster**.
Tom runs the **fastest**.

fasten

Fasten the rope to the sled.
Join the rope to the sled.

fat, fatter, fattest

1. All the pigs are **fat**.
They are well covered with
flesh.
The black one is **fatter**
than the pink one. The
spotted pig is the **fattest**.
2. **Fat** is a food.
Fat is found in milk, butter,
meat and other foods.

father

Children have a mother
and a **father**. The **father**
is a man.
My **father** loves his children.

faucet

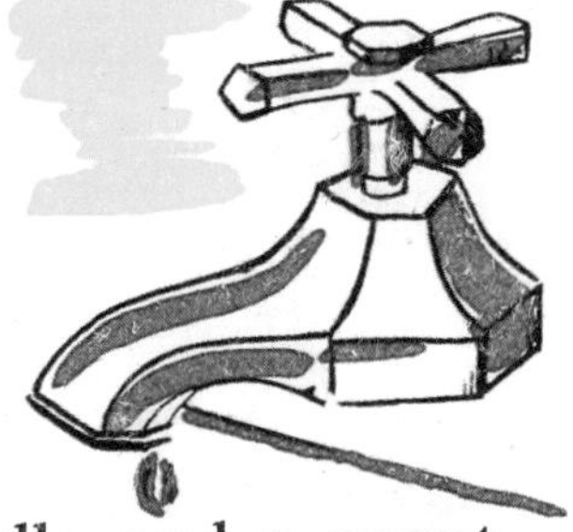

A **faucet** is
an inven-
tion for
drawing
water.
It has a handle and a spout.

F G H I J K L M N O P Q R S T U V W X Y Z

find, finding, found

Roy will **find** the ball.
He is looking for it
and he will see it.
Roy is always **finding**
things for people.
Now he has found the ball.

fine

1. The wire is **fine.**
The wire is thin.
2. It is a **fine** day.
The day is sunny and clear.
3. The man drove too fast.
He had to pay a **fine.**
He had to pay money
as a punishment.

finger, fingers

A **finger** is a
part of the hand.
The four **fingers** on the
hand are of different lengths.

fingernail, fingernails

A **fingernail** is the hard
part on the end of a
finger.
Rose has red
fingernails.

finish

We **finish** eating lunch
before we go out to play.
We come to the end of lunch
before we go out to play.

fir

The **fir** tree
is an
evergreen.
Its leaves are like needles.

fire

1. When things burn,
we have a **fire.**
The cat likes the hot **fire.**
2. Bob will
fire
his rifle.
He will make the rifle go off.

fire engine, firemen

The **fire engine** is a
vehicle which carries
firemen and their tools
to the fire.
The **firemen** put out the fire.

fireplace

A **fireplace** is a place
where a fire is built.
Our **fireplace** is made of brick.

firm

1. Andrew works for a book **firm**.
He works for a book company.
2. The post is **firm**.
It cannot be moved.

first

1. Philip is **first** in line.
He is at the head of the line.
2. This is my **first** muff.
I have never had one before.

fish, fishes

A **fish** is an animal.
Fishes live in the water.
Many **fish** are good to eat.

fishing, fisherman, fishermen

This man is **fishing**.
He is catching fish.
He is a **fisherman**.

Some **fishermen** go out to sea to catch fish.

fist

A closed hand is called a **fist**.

fit

Mother's shoes do not **fit** me. They are too large for my feet.

five

I have **five** jacks and a ball.
Five is a number.
3 and 2 are 5.

fix

Peter's truck is broken.
Daddy will **fix** it.
Daddy will mend it.

flag

The Scout has a **flag**.
A **flag** is made of cloth.
A **flag** has a design with a special meaning.
The **flag** of the United States has stars and stripes.

flow

The rivers **flow** to the sea.
The rivers run into the sea.

flower, flowers

A **flower** is the blossom of a plant.
Flowers produce seeds.
These are **flowers**:

rose

pansy

daisy

violet

buttercup

tulip

fly, flies

A **fly** is an insect.
Flies carry disease germs.

fly, flying, flew, flown

The birds **fly** easily.
They go through the air.
They are **flying** away from me.
One bird **flew** to the tree.
Another has **flown** after it.

fold

Fold the paper to make a fan.
Bend the paper over on itself.

follow

Spot will **follow** Tom to school.
Spot will go after Tom.

follower

The knight was a **follower** of the king.
The knight obeyed the king's commands.

fond

Jane is **fond** of her kitten.
She likes her kitten.

food

Things that we eat are called **food**.
Food keeps us alive.
Food makes us grow.

fool

A **fool**
is a person without sense.
Kings used to keep a **fool**
at court to amuse people.

foolish

Edwin told a **foolish** story.
The story did not make sense.

foot, feet

1. A **foot**
is a measure of length.
Twelve inches make a **foot**.

2. A **foot** is
part of the
body.
We stand on
our **feet**.

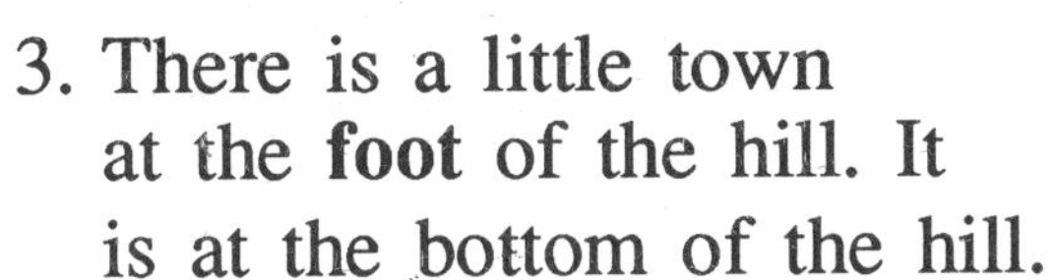

3. There is a little town
at the **foot** of the hill. It
is at the bottom of the hill.

football

1. A **football**
is a leather ball.
It is filled with air.

2. **Football** is a game.
The players kick the ball.

for

1. Dad went **for** the paper.
Dad went to get the paper.
2. The gift was **for** Tom.
It was given to Tom.

forbid

Mother did **forbid** me to go.
She did tell me not to go.

force

1. A **force** is a group of men.
The police **force** are men
who keep order in the
city.

2. **Force** is strength used
to do some kind of work.
The men used **force**
to open the door.

forehead

The **forehead** is part of the
face between the hair
and the eyes.

Dad's glasses are
on his **forehead**.

F G H I J K L M N O P Q R S T U V W X Y Z

fourth

Pete has picked three apples.
He will pick a **fourth** one now.

fowl, fowls

A **fowl** is a bird.
Fowls are kept on a farm.
They lay eggs for us to eat.
They are used for meat.
A chicken is a **fowl**.

fox, foxes

A **fox** is a wild animal.
It looks like a dog.
Foxes have thick tails.

fraction

1. A **fraction** is one or more parts of a whole number.
   $\frac{3}{5}$ is a **fraction**.

The whole number has five parts.
Three of these parts have been taken to make the **fraction**.

2. A **fraction** is a piece of anything.

fragrant

The flowers are **fragrant**.
They smell sweet.

frail

The vase is **frail**.
It is not strong.
It can be broken easily.

frame

1. The **frame** is the part of a thing that gives it shape and strength.

Sometimes the **frame** of a building is made of steel.
Sometimes it is made of wood.

2. A **frame** is the part around the edge of a picture.

frank

Jimmy is **frank.**
He says what he thinks.

free, freedom

1. The entertainment is **free**.
It does not cost anything.

2. Slaves are not **free**.
They cannot do as they choose.
Prisoners are not **free**.
They cannot go where they choose.
Free people can act and speak as they choose.
They ought to use their **freedom** wisely.

freeze, freezing, froze, frozen

The pond will **freeze** in winter.
The water will turn into ice.
It **froze** last week.
We like to see it **freezing**.
When it has **frozen**,
we can skate on the ice.

freight

1. **Freight** is the cost of carrying goods by train or boat.
2. The goods that are carried are called **freight**.
3. The **freight** train carries milk, grain, cattle, and other things we need.

frequent

We had **frequent** showers.
We had many showers, with little time between them.

fresh

We like **fresh** eggs.

We like new eggs that the hens have just laid.

fret, frets

Why does the baby **fret**?
Why does he complain?
He is not comfortable.

friction

A match lights by **friction**.

It lights when it is rubbed against something.

friend

Joan is my **friend**.
I like Joan.
I like to play with her.

friendly

Ruffles is a **friendly** dog.
He likes everybody.

F
G
H
I
J
K
L
M
N
O
P
Q
R
S
T
U
V
W
X
Y
Z

furnace

A **furnace** is a large stove.
A **furnace** heats our house.

furnish

1. Mother will **furnish** ice cream for the party.
Mother will give the ice cream.
2. Gloria plans to **furnish** her new home.
She plans to put furniture into it.

furniture

Things that we use in a house are called **furniture**.

further

John does not need **further** help.
He does not need any more help.

G g

gain

The pencil cost us four pence.
We sell it for five pence.
Our **gain** is one pence.
That is our profit.

gale

A **gale** is a strong wind.

gallon

A **gallon** is liquid measure.
Four quarts make a **gallon**.

gallop

A **gallop** is a quick run.
The hunters chase a fox.
Their horses **gallop**.

galoshes

Galoshes are rubber overshoes.
Alice is wearing **galoshes**.

game

We play a **game** by rules.
The boys are playing a **game**.
It is a ball **game**.

Mother likes a **game** of cards.

gap

There is a **gap** in the fence.
There is an open space.

garage

1. A **garage** is a building.
We keep the car in a **garage**.

2. We take the car to a **garage** when it needs to be fixed.

garbage, garbage can

Bits of food not used are **garbage**.
Bones and peels are **garbage**.
They go into the **garbage can**.

garden, gardener

A **garden** is land on which flowers and vegetables grow.
Peter is planting a **garden**.
He is a **gardener**.

garment, garments

A **garment** is a piece of clothing.
The prince had fine **garments**.

gas, gases

A **gas** is a substance like air.
Some **gases** burn.

This is a **gas** stove.

This is a **gas** light.

generous

Grandfather is **generous.**
He is kind to people.
He likes to make gifts.

gentle

Ted's pony is **gentle.**
Ted's pony is tame and quiet.

gentleman, gentlemen

The **gentleman** gave the lady his seat on the bus.
Gentlemen have good manners.

genuine

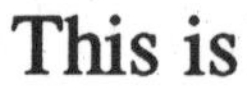

This is a **genuine** leather bag.
It is made of real leather.

geography

Geography is the study of the earth, with its people, plants, animals, climates, places, and products.

geranium

A **geranium** plant has a pretty flower.
Anna has a red **geranium.**

germ, germs

A **germ** is a tiny living thing.
Germs cause diseases.
Mother boiled the jars.
Boiling killed the **germs.**

get, getting, got

Peter will **get** carrots from his garden.
He will take the carrots and bring them home.
He is **getting** fresh vegetables each day.
Yesterday he **got** beans from his garden.

giant

Jack saw a **giant.**
Jack saw a big man.

glare

1. A **glare** is a strong light.
2. A **glare** is an angry look.

glass, glasses

Glass is a hard material.
It is easy to break.
Light passes through **glass**.

The windowpane
is made of **glass**.

These are drinking **glasses**.
They are made of **glass**.

Dad wears **glasses** for reading.
They are made of
a special kind of **glass**.

glide

The model plane can **glide**
on a current of air.
It goes smoothly.

glider

A **glider** is an aeroplane
without an engine.

globe

A **globe** is shaped like a
ball.
This **globe**
has the
map of
the earth
on it.

glorious

We won a **glorious** victory.
It was a great victory.
It made us proud.

glove, gloves

A **glove** is a covering
for the hand.
Mother has white **gloves**.

Bob has boxing **gloves**.

glow

Electric heaters **glow**.
They have no flame.
They give light and heat.

glue

Glue is a sticky material.
The parts of the toy are
held together by **glue**.

gnaw

Scrappy will **gnaw** the bone.
He will chew on the bone.

go, goes, going, went, gone

I **go** to school.
Tom **goes** to school.
We walk from our home
to the schoolhouse.
We are **going** together.
Yesterday I **went** late.
Tom had **gone** earlier.

goat

A **goat** is an animal.
A **goat** has horns.

gobble, gobbles

1. Spot will **gobble** food.
He eats fast and noisily.
2. The turkey **gobbles**.
He makes a funny noise.

gold

Gold is a valuable metal.
It is made into money.
It is made
into pins
and rings.

golden

The goose laid **golden** eggs.
The eggs were made of gold.
The clouds were **golden**.
They were the colour of gold.

goldenrod

Goldenrod is
a yellow
flower.

goldfish

Beatrice has
two **goldfish**
in a glass
bowl.

golf

Golf is a game, played
with a ball and sticks.

grace

We say **grace** before meals.
We say a short prayer before eating.

grade

1. I am in the third **grade**.
I am in the third year at school.

2. We drove up the **grade**.
We drove up the hill.

graduate

Twenty pupils will **graduate** the university in June.
They will finish the work of the university in June.

grain, grains

wheat rye corn

1. **Grain** is a kind of grass.
We eat the seeds of **grains**.
2. A **grain** is a tiny piece.
There are many **grains** of sand on the beach.

grammar

We study **grammar**.
We learn the rules of speaking and writing our language correctly.

grand

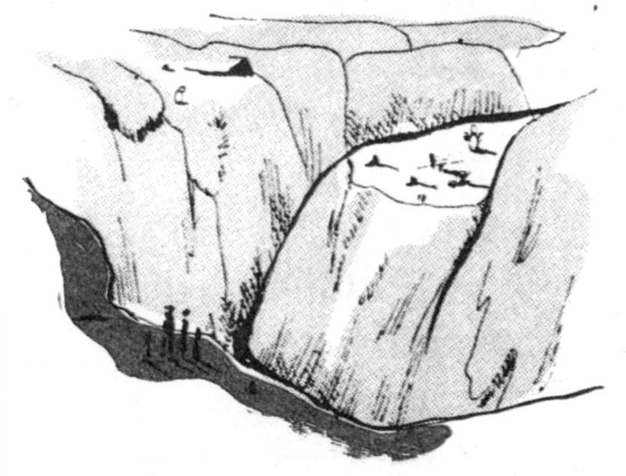

Grand means great, beautiful, or important.
We saw the **Grand** Canyon.

This is a **grand** piano.

grandfather, grandpa

I have two **grandfathers**.
One **grandfather** is my mother's father.
The other **grandfather** is my father's father.
I call them both **grandpa**.

grandma, grandmother

I have two **grandmothers**.
One **grandmother**
is my mother's mother.
The other **grandmother**
is my father's mother.
Grandma Day has white hair.

grapes

Grapes are a fruit.
Some **grapes** are purple
and some **grapes** are green.

grapefruit

Grapefruit
is a fruit.
It is large and yellow.

grass, grasses

Grass is a green plant.
It has long, narrow leaves.
Grass grows on a lawn.
There are many wild **grasses**.

grasshopper

The **grasshopper**
is an insect.
It has long legs for jumping.

grateful

We are **grateful** for your
help.
We are pleased.
We thank you.

grave

1. A **grave** is a place in
the earth where dead
bodies are laid to rest.
2. Grandpa's
face is
grave.

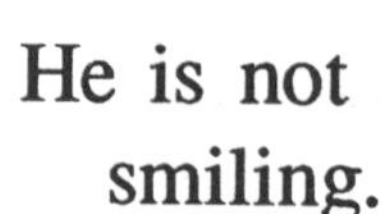

He is not
smiling.

gravel

The path is covered with
gravel.
It is covered with
small stones.

gravy

Gravy is a liquid
food.
It is made from meat
juices.
We pour **gravy** over our
meat.

grind, grinder, ground

We saw the man **grind** the coffee beans in the big **grinder**. He **ground** them into small pieces.

grocer, grocery, groceries

The **grocer** sells food.
He has a **grocery** store.
Groceries are sold in cans and packages.

gross

A **gross** is twelve dozen.

ground

Peter digs the **ground** to make a garden.
He turns over the earth.

group

A **group** is a number of people or a number of things.
Dad took a **group** picture.
Dad took a picture of several people together.

grove

There is a **grove** of trees on the side of the hill.
There is a group of trees on the side of the hill.

grow, growing, grew, grown

Children **grow** each year.
They become larger each year.
Tom is **growing** fast.
He **grew** three inches last year.
Rose has **grown** up.

growl
Spot will **growl** at Inkie.
He will make a low,
angry sound in his throat.

grunt

Pigs **grunt**.
They make a low, deep
noise in their throats.

guard

A **guard** watches against
danger.
The life **guard** on the
beach sees that we are safe.

guess, guesses

Guess what
I have
in my
hand.
Try to think what I have.
You may have three **guesses**.

guest
Aunt Jackie is our **guest**.
She is staying with us awhile.

guide
Sam does not know the way.
Tom will **guide** him.
Tom will show him the way.

gulf

A **gulf** is a stretch
of water from the sea.
It has land on three sides.

gum
1. The **gum** is part of the
mouth in which teeth grow.
2. **Gum** is a sticky material.
Many people chew a **gum**
which has a pleasant flavour.

gun, guns
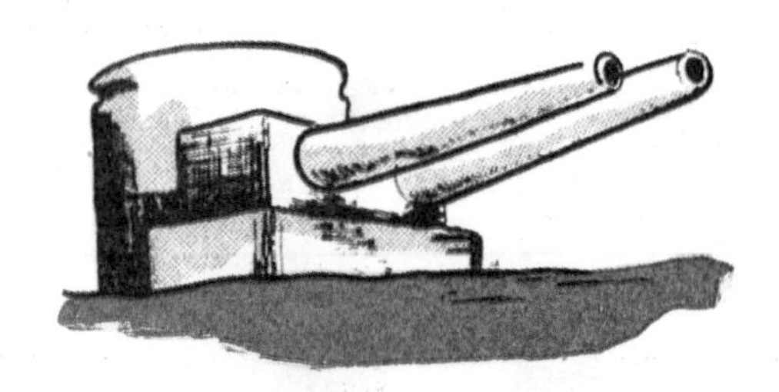
A **gun** is a weapon.
It has a metal pipe.
It shoots balls of metal.
The ship has big **guns**.

G H I J K L M N O P Q R S T U V W X Y Z

H h

habit

A **habit** is a thing that we do again and again.
Laura has a good **habit**.
She rises early every day.

hail

1. Andrew will **hail** a taxi.
He will call to the driver.
2. **Hail** falls like rain.
Small balls of ice fall from the sky.

hair

Hair grows on the skin.
It is like fine threads.
Sally is brushing her **hair**.

half, halves

A **half** is one of the two equal parts of anything.
The apple has two **halves**.

hall

1. A **hall** is a room just inside the door.

2. A **hall** is a passageway in a building.
3. A **hall** is a building with a large room used for meetings.
4. A large public room is called a **hall**.

ham

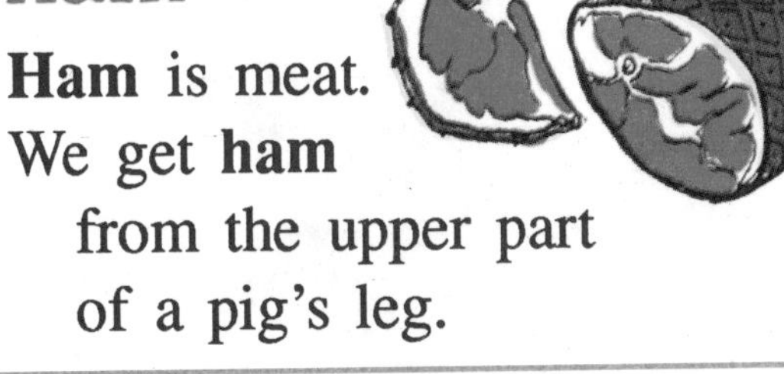

Ham is meat.
We get **ham** from the upper part of a pig's leg.

hammer

A **hammer** is a tool.
John is making a box.
He hits nails with a **hammer**.

hamper

A **hamper** is a picnic basket. We fill it with food when we have a picnic.

hand

1. A **hand** is part of the body.

Tony holds a ball in his **hand**.

2. A **hand** is part of a clock.

The long **hand** of the clock points to the minutes.
The short **hand** of the clock points to the hours.

3. Please **hand** me a cup.

Pass it to me with your **hand**.

handful

Pat has a **handful** of nuts.
He has as many nuts as his hand can hold.

handkerchief

A **handkerchief** is a piece of cloth or paper used for blowing the nose.

handle, handles

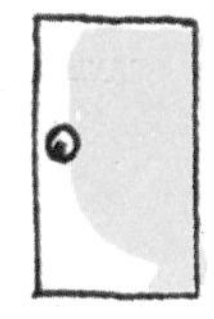

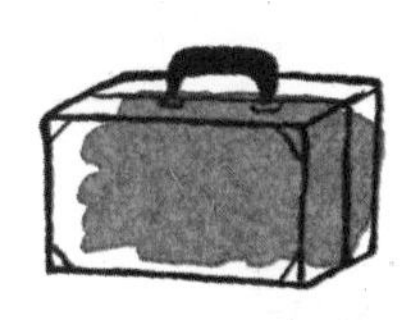

We hold things by the **handle**.
The knife, the door, and the suitcase all have **handles**.

handsome

Dick is a **handsome** boy.
He is a good-looking boy.

hang, hanging, hung

Dad will **hang** the picture.
He will put it on a hook.
He is **hanging** the picture above the table.
He has **hung** it straight.

hangar

A **hangar** is a building in which aeroplanes are kept.

haste

We must make **haste.**
We must go quickly.

hat

A **hat** is worn on the head.
Ann's **hat** has a ribbon.

hatch

The hen sits on her eggs to keep them warm.
Soon she will **hatch** chicks.
Little chickens will come out of the eggs.

hatchet

A **hatchet** is a small axe.
It has a short handle.

hate

Hate is a strong feeling of dislike.
Many people **hate** war.

haul

The horse will **haul** the load.
The horse will pull the load.

having, had have, has

1. I **have** a ball.
The ball is in my hand.

Terry **has** a bat.
We are **having** a game.
We wish that we **had** more players.
2. We **have** a motor car.
We own a motor car.

hawk, hawks

A **hawk** is a bird.
Some **hawks** catch chickens.

hay, haystack

Hay is dried grass.
Some animals eat **hay**.
The **hay** is piled in a **haystack**.

he

Tom is my brother.
He (Tom) is ten years old.

head

1. A **head** is part of a body.
We are putting a **head** on the snowman.
2. This is a **head** of cabbage.
3. Joe is at the **head** of the line.
He is first in line.
4. Dad is the **head** of a business. Dad is the owner of the business.

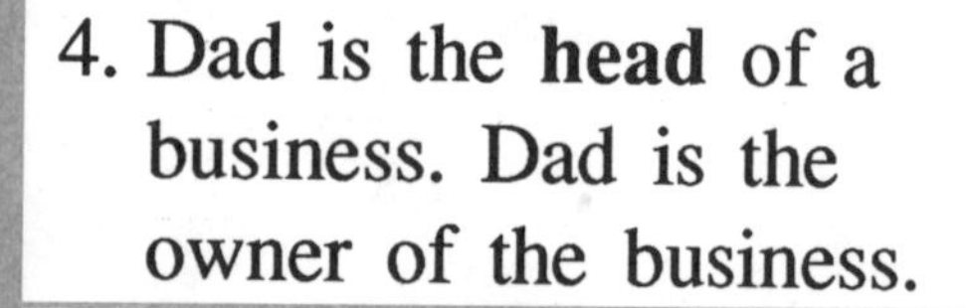

heal

The cut will **heal** quickly.
It will get well quickly.

headache

Mother has a **headache**.
She has a pain in her head.

health, healthy

Baby has good **health**.
Baby is **healthy**.
He is never sick.
He is strong and well.

heap

This is a **heap** of coal.
This is a pile of coal.

hear, hearing, heard

Grandpa does not **hear** well.
Grandpa's **hearing** is poor.
His ears do not get sounds clearly.
He has not **heard** what you said.

heart

The **heart** is a part of the body.
The **heart** is in the chest.
It is a pump. It sends blood through the body.

heat

1. **Heat** is warm.
We feel the **heat** that comes from the sun.
Fire makes **heat**.
2. We **heat** the house in cold weather.
We have a fire to make the house warm.

heavy, heavier, heaviest

Tom has a **heavy** bag.
The bag is hard to lift.
Mother carries a **heavier** bag.
Dad carries the **heaviest** bag.

hedge

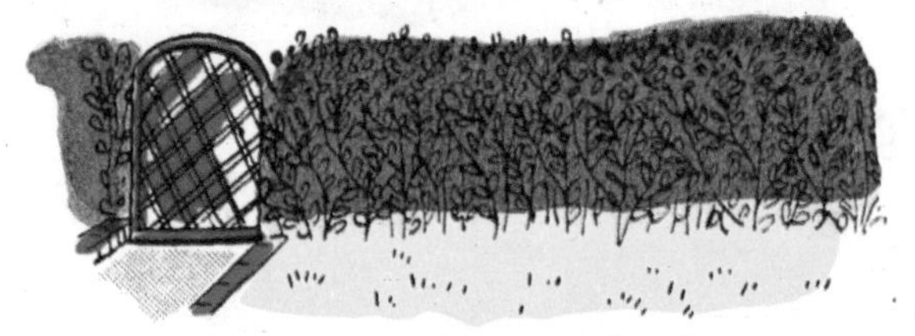

A **hedge** is a line of plants.
It is used as a fence.
Dad is clipping the **hedge**.

heel, heels

1. The **heel** is the back of the foot.
2. A **heel** is part of a shoe.

These shoes have high **heels**.

height

Helen is four feet in **height**.
She is four feet tall.

help

I **help** mother peel potatoes.
I do some of her work.

hem

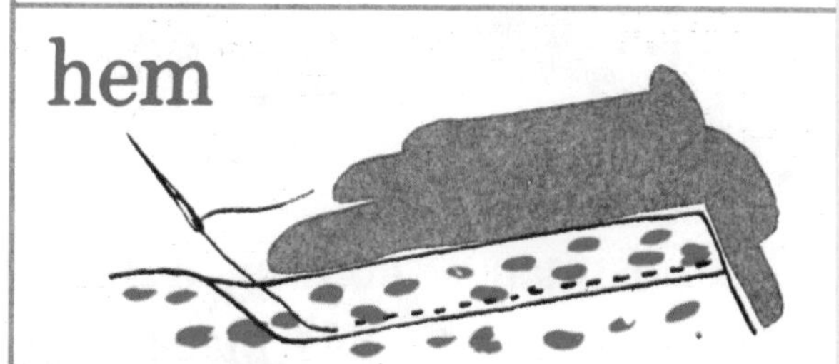

This is the way to make a **hem**.
The cloth is folded over and sewed neatly.

hen

A **hen** is a fowl.
A **hen** lays eggs.

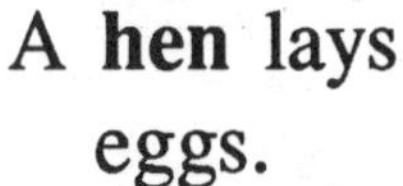

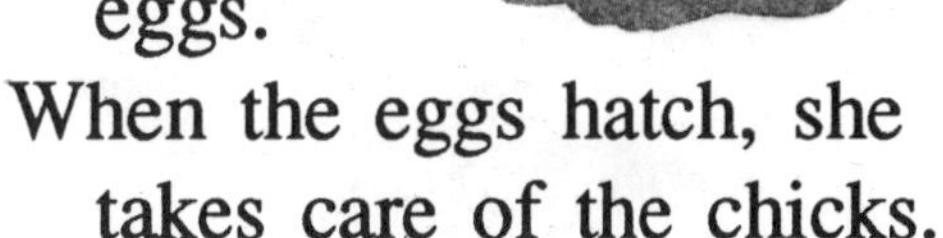

When the eggs hatch, she takes care of the chicks.

her

Mary says this is **her** pen.
The pen belongs to **her** (Mary).

herd

A **herd** is a number of animals kept together.
This is a **herd** of goats.

here

The postman is coming **here**.
He is coming to this place.

hero, heroes, heroine

A **hero** is a brave man.
We like stories about **heroes**.
A brave woman
is called a **heroine**.

herself

Nobody
helped
the Little Red Hen.
She planted the grain **herself**.

hide, hiding, hid, hidden

We shall all **hide**.
We shall go out of sight.
I am **hiding** behind the sofa.
Tom **hid** in the closet.
Ann is **hidden** somewhere, too.

hide, hides

A **hide** is
the skin of an animal.
Leather is made from **hides**.

high, higher, highest

The mountains are **high**.
They are far above us.
They are **higher** than the
hills.
Do you see the **highest** peak?

hike

We took a **hike**.
We took a long walk
in the country.

hill

A **hill** is high land.
A **hill** is not so high as a
mountain.

him

Give Tom's knife to **him**.
Give the knife to **him** (Tom).

himself

Sam wrote the letter **himself**.
No one wrote it for him.

hinge, hinges

The door has a **hinge**.
The **hinge** joins the door
to the frame of the door.
The door swings on its **hinges**.

hip, hips

A **hip** is a joint where
the leg joins the body.
Jayne has
her hands
on her
hips.

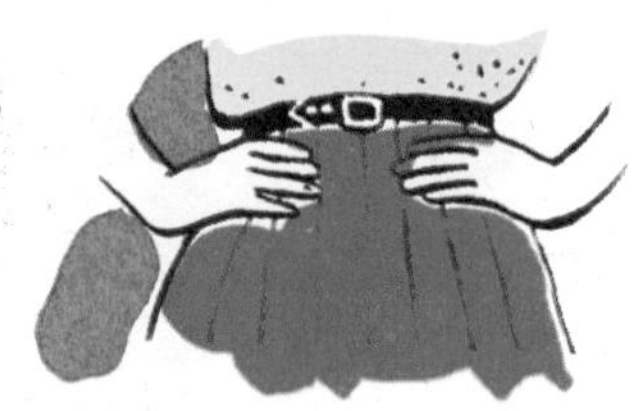

hire

Jim will **hire** John to help
him.
He will pay John for his work.

his

Spot lost **his** ball.
It was **his** (Spot's) own ball.

history

We like stories of **history**.
They are true stories about
things that once happened.

hit

Bill threw a snowball.
It **hit** Mr. Purdy's hat.
It struck Mr. Purdy's hat.

hive

A **hive** is a
little
house
in which bees are kept.

hoarse

The man's voice is **hoarse**.
It is rough and heavy.

hoe

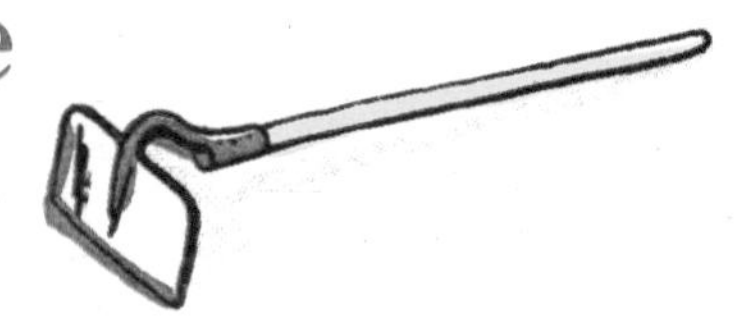

A **hoe** is a garden tool.
It is used to dig up weeds
and to loosen the earth.

hog

A **hog** is a pig.

horseshoe

A **horseshoe** is an iron shoe made to fit a horse's hoof.

hose

1. A **hose** is a rubber pipe. Dad is watering the lawn with a **hose**.
2. Stockings are sometimes called **hose**.

hospital

A **hospital** is a building where sick people get care.

host, hostess

Jerry is **host** at his party.
When Sally gives a party, she is the **hostess**.

hot

The cocoa is **hot**.
It burns my tongue.

hotel

A **hotel** is a building where people may hire a room and buy meals.

hound

A **hound** is a hunting dog.
Rover is a **hound**.
He has long ears and a good sense of smell.

hour, hours

An **hour** is a measure of time.
An **hour** has sixty minutes.
A day has twenty-four **hours**.

house

A **house** is a building in which people live.
This is Jack's **house**.

how

How does the lift work?
In what way does it work?

H I J K L M N O P Q R S T U V W X Y Z

hurry, hurrying, hurried

We **hurry** when we are late.
We go fast.
We are **hurrying** to school.
We have **hurried** all the way.

hurt

Dorothy is **hurt**.
She is crying with pain.

husband

Rose and Andrew are married.
Andrew is her **husband**.

hush

Hush! Be quiet, or you will awaken the baby.

husk

A **husk** is the cover of a fruit or seed.
An ear of corn has a **husk**.

hut

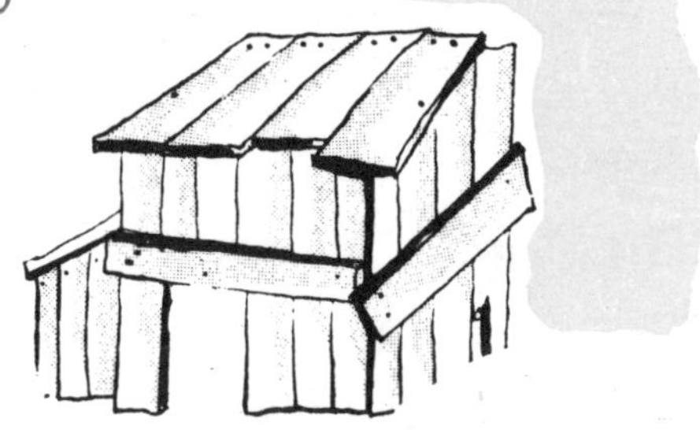

The boys have built a **hut**.
They have built a little house.

I i

I

George says, "**I** know the answer!"

ice

Ice is frozen water.
It is hard and cold.

icebox

An **icebox** is a refrigerator.
We keep food in it to keep it fresh.

ice cream

Ice cream is a frozen food.
It is made of cream, sugar, and other things.

icicle

Water dropping from the
roof has turned into ice.
It has made an **icicle**.
Ice hangs in a pointed stick.

icy

The pavement is **icy**.
It is covered with ice.

idea

I had an **idea** for a story.
The thought was in my mind.

idle

Harry is **idle**.
He is not doing anything.

if

1. **If** Ruth were older,
she could be a Girl Guide.
She is not yet old enough.
2. See **if** the door is shut.
See whether or not it is shut.

ignorant

I am **ignorant** about cooking.
I know nothing about cooking.

ill, illness

Mandy is **ill**.
She has an **illness**.
She is sick.

illustrate

Jayne has written a story.
Now she will **illustrate** it.
She will draw pictures
about the story.

imagine

Sam likes to
imagine that he is a horse.
He pretends that he is a
horse.

immediately

You should come **immediately**.
You should come this minute.

immense

1. The public library has an
immense number of books.
It has a great number
of books.
2. The building is **immense**.
It is very large.

invent, invention, inventor

Eli Whitney worked to
invent a way to remove
seeds from cotton.
He made an **invention**.
He was an **inventor**.
An **inventor** finds a new
way to make or do
something.

invitation, invite

Send Alice an **invitation**.
Invite her to come.
Ask her to come.

iron

1. **Iron** is a metal.
Horse shoes are made of **iron**.
Chains are made of **iron**.
2. We press clothes
with an **iron**.

irrigate

Farmers **irrigate** dry land
by means of water
running through ditches.

is

Edward **is** my cousin.
He **is** tall and strong.
He **is** working on a farm.

island

An **island** is land
with water on all sides.

isthmus

An **isthmus** is a narrow
piece of land.
It joins two larger
pieces of land.

it

This is my umbrella.
It is a small umbrella.

its

A bird has **its** nest
in the apple tree.
The nest of the bird
is in the apple tree.

itself

Somebody moved my chair.
It cannot move by **itself**.

J j

jack, jacks

1. A **jack** is a tool used for raising a car.
2. This card is the **Jack** of Hearts.

3. The Union **Jack** is a flag.

4. We play a game with **jacks** and a ball.

jacket

Dot's **jacket** is blue.
A **jacket** is a short coat.

jack-o'-lantern

Tom has made a **jack-o'-lantern.**
He made it from a pumpkin.

jail

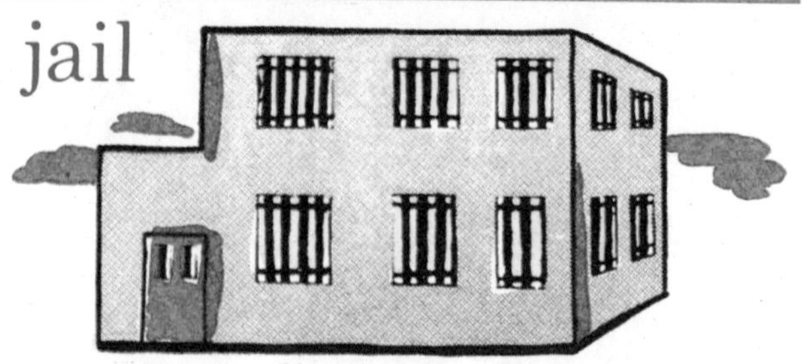

A **jail** is a prison.
People who do wrong are sometimes put into **jail**.

jam

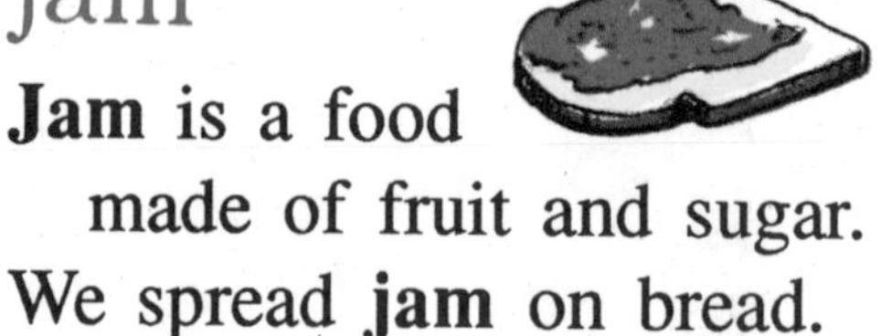

Jam is a food made of fruit and sugar.
We spread **jam** on bread.

janitor

A **janitor** is a man who takes care of a building.

jar

1. The pickles are in a **jar.**
2. The thunder seemed to **jar** the house.
   It seemed to shake the house.

jaw, jaws

The **jaw** is a bone in the face.
We have two **jaws**.
Teeth grow in the **jaws**.

jeep

A **jeep** is an army car.

jelly

Jelly is a food.
It is made of fruit juice and sugar.

jerk

The train started with a **jerk**.
It made a sudden start.

jewel, jewels,

A **jewel** is a precious stone.
A ruby is a **jewel**.
Jewels are made to be worn as ornaments.

job

Jimmy has a **job**.
He has regular work.
He is paid for his work.

join

We all **join** hands.
We put our hands together.

joint, joints

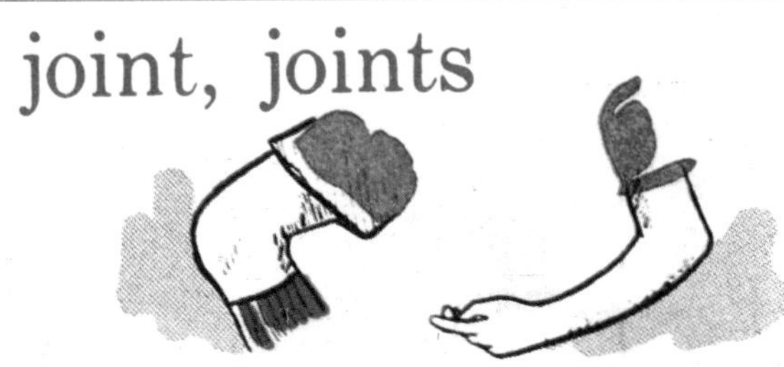

A **joint** is part of the body where two bones join.
We bend at our **joints**.
The knee is a **joint**.
The elbow is a **joint**.

joke

A **joke** is a funny story or a funny trick.

jolly

Santa Claus is **jolly**.
He is full of fun.

journey

Father took a **journey**.
He went on a trip.

joy, joyful

Joy is happiness.
We laugh with **joy**.
We are **joyful**.
We are full of **joy**.

judge, judges

1. In a court of law, the **judge** sends people to jail, or makes them pay a fine for doing wrong.

2. A **judge** makes a decision.
The **judges** at the dog show said that Ruffles was the best dog.

judgement

Bob has good **judgement**.
He has good sense.

juice, juicy

Juice is a liquid.
We squeeze **juice** from oranges.
Oranges are **juicy**.
They are full of **juice**.

jump

Dick can **jump** over the fence.
He can go over the fence.

junk

1. Old things which are thrown away are called **junk**.

2. A **junk** is a Chinese ship.

jury, juries

A **jury** is a group of people in a court of law.
Juries decide whether or not a person has done a crime.

just

1. The judge is **just**.
He gives a fair decision.
2. I have **just** come.
I came this minute.

justice

The man asked for **justice**.
He asked for fair treatment.

K k

kangaroo

A **kangaroo** is an animal
with strong legs for jumping.

keen

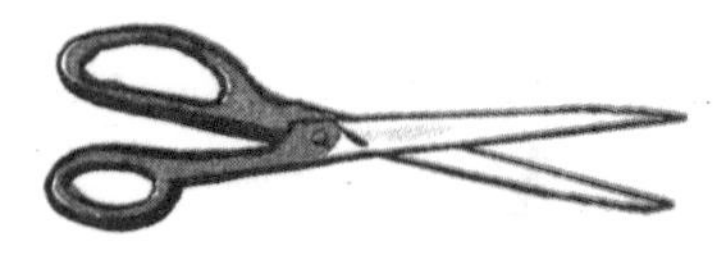

The scissors are **keen**.
They are very sharp.

keep, keeping, kept

I **keep** all my pennies.
I save them.
I am **keeping** them to buy
Christmas gifts.
I have **kept** them in my bank.

kernel

1. A **kernel** is the seed of a grain.
2. A **kernel** is the part of a nut inside the shell.

We eat the **kernel**.

kerosene

Kerosene is oil made from petroleum.
Kerosene is used as fuel for stoves and lamps.

kettle

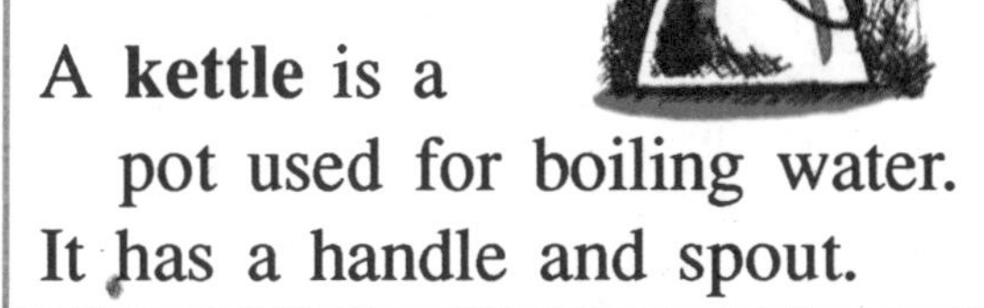

A **kettle** is a pot used for boiling water.
It has a handle and spout.

key, keyhole, keyboard

1. This is a **key**.

A **key** fits into a **keyhole**, and locks or unlocks a door.

2. The typewriter has a **key** for each letter and sign.

This is the **keyboard**.

3. A **key** is a low island.

kick

Joe will **kick** the football.
He will strike it with his foot.

kid

A **kid** is a young goat.

The hide of a **kid** is used to make **kid** gloves and shoes.

kill

Cats **kill** mice.
They put mice to death.

kind, kindness

1. We are **kind** to our pets.
We treat them with **kindness**.
We do not hurt them.
2. What **kind** of bird is that?
What sort of bird is that?

kindergarten

When we first go to school, we are in **kindergarten**.
It is a class for very young girls and boys.

king, kingdom

A **king** is a ruler.
His country is a **kingdom**.

kiss, kisses

1. Ann will **kiss** Dad good night.

kitchen

The **kitchen** is a room in which food is cooked.

kite

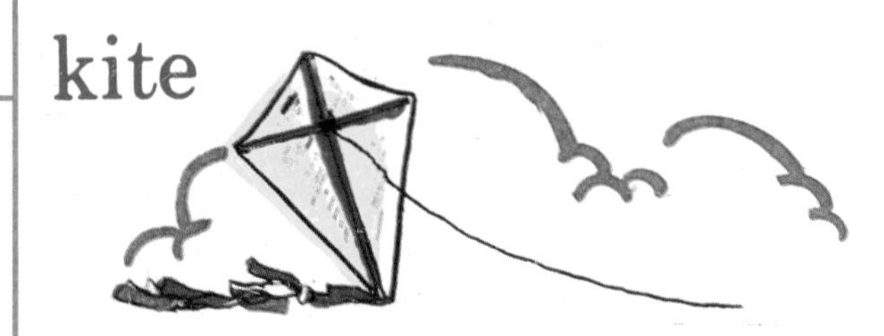

A **kite** is a toy.
Ronald is flying a **kite**.

kitten

A **kitten** is a young cat.

knee, knees, kneels

A **knee** is part of the body.
It is the joint between the upper and lower leg.
Ruth is on her **knees**.
She **kneels** to pray.

K L M N O P Q R S T U V W X Y Z

knife, knives

A **knife** has a blade.
It is used for cutting.
These are **knives**.

knight

In days of old, a **knight**
was a man of noble birth
who fought for his king.

knit

Mother **knit** Tom a sweater.
She used yarn and long needles.

knob

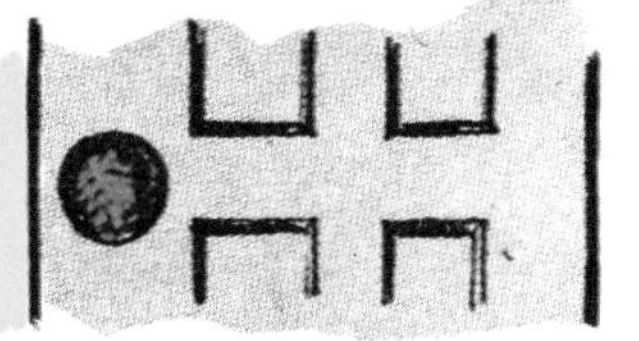

A **knob** is a round thing.
The handle of the door
is called a door **knob**.

knock, knocked

1. John will **knock** at the door.
He will rap on the door with his hand.
2. Sam will **knock** the ball with his baseball bat.
Sam will strike the ball.
3. Baby **knocked** his head against the table.
He bumped his head against the table.

knot

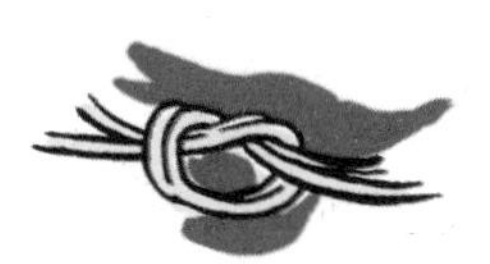

Harry tied the rope in a **knot**.
It was a square **knot**.

know, knowing, knew, known

Spot stole some meat.
Spot, you **know** better.
Spot is a **knowing** dog.
He **knew** that he did wrong. He understood that he did wrong.
He must have **known** that we would punish him.

knowledge

At school we get **knowledge**.
We learn many things.

L l

label

A **label** is on the jar.
It tells what is in the jar.

labour

Labour is hard work.
Painting the house is **labour**.

lace, laces

1. **Lace** is a fine material made of threads.

Lois has a **lace** collar.

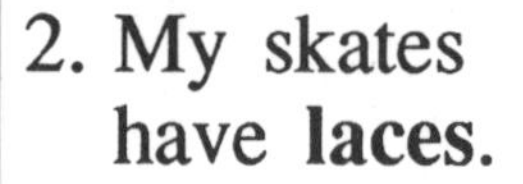

2. My skates have **laces**.

Cords go through holes and are pulled to fasten the skates.

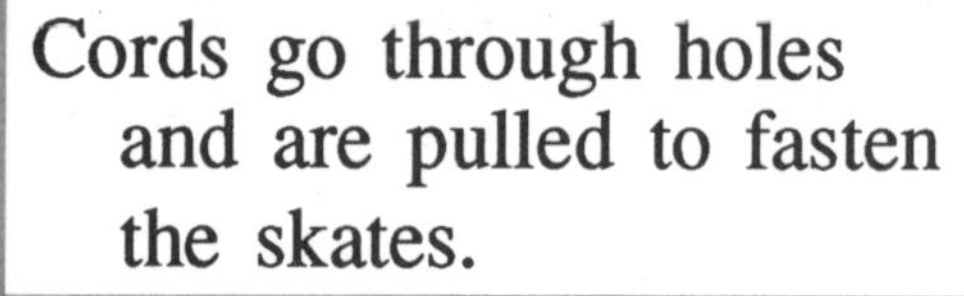

lack

We **lack** one book.
We need one more book.

ladder, ladders

A **ladder** is a set of steps used for climbing.
These are **ladders**.

lady, ladies

Mother is a tall **lady**.
Ann is a little **lady**.
Ladies have good manners.

lake

A **lake** is a stretch of water with land on all sides.
Our cabin is beside a **lake**.

lamb

A **lamb** is the young of a sheep.

lame

The soldier is **lame**.
His foot has been hurt.

L
M
N
O
P
Q
R
S
T
U
V
W
X
Y
Z

late
School begins at nine. Ann came in two minutes after nine. Ann was **late**.

lately
I have not seen Ted **lately**.
I have not seen Ted for a long time.

latter
1. It rained at the **latter** part of the week. It rained at the end of the week.
2. Tom and Bob are brothers.
The **latter** is older.
The second one named is older.

laugh

The picture was funny.
It made people **laugh** out loud.

laundry
1. **Laundry** is clothing ready to be washed.
2. A **laundry** is a place where clothing is washed.

law
A **law** is a rule about the right way to act.
A **law** is made by the government.

lawn

A **lawn** is a stretch of grass.
Grass on the lawn is cut.
The **lawn** is smooth.

lawyer
A **lawyer** is a person who earns his living by the knowledge of law.

lay, laying, laid
We **lay** dishes on the table.
We put them down on the table.
We are **laying** the silver beside the plates. We **laid** a napkin by each place.

lazy
Harry is **lazy**.
He does not wish to work.

L M N O P Q R S T U V W X Y Z

leather

Leather is made from hides.
Leather is used to make shoes, bags, and many other things.

leave, leaving, left

1. We had to **leave** early.
We had to go away early.
The clock struck the hour just as we were **leaving**.
We **left** at eight o'clock.
2. Dad gave me **leave** to go.
He said I might go.
3. **Leave** the book on the table. Let it stay there.

left

Pat writes with his **left** hand.

leg, legs

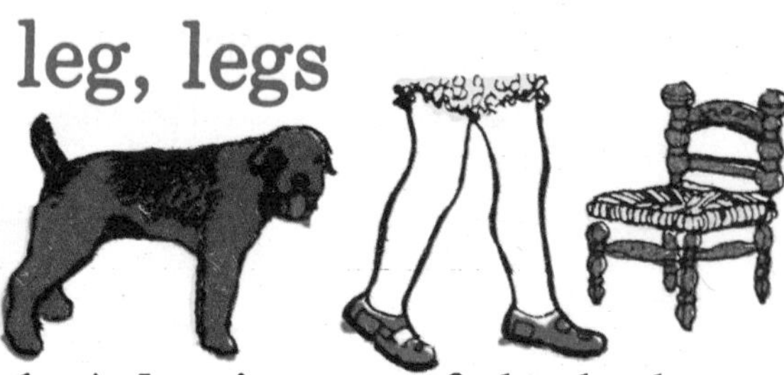

1. A **leg** is part of the body.
We stand and walk with our **legs**.
A person has two **legs**.
A dog has four **legs**.
2. A chair stands on four **legs**.

lemon, lemonade

A **lemon** is a sour fruit.
We make **lemonade** of **lemon** juice, sugar, and water.

lend

The library will **lend** books.
We must take the books back.

length

The **length** of the box is ten inches.
The box is ten inches long.

less

1. Tom has **less** money than I.
Tom has a smaller amount.
2. 5 **less** 3 leaves 2.
3 taken from 5 leaves 2.

lesson

Grace has one music **lesson** a week.
She is taught music for one hour each week.

L M N O P Q R S T U V W X Y Z

let

1. The house is to **let**.
It is for rent.
2. **Let** me do it.
Allow me to do it.

letter, letters

1. A **letter** is a sign used in writing and printing.
A, B, and C are **letters**.
2. A **letter** is a written message sent by one person to another.

lettuce

Lettuce is a vegetable.
It has green leaves.
It is used in salads.

level

The tennis court is **level**.
It is flat and even.

liberty

Liberty means freedom.

library, libraries

A **library** is a room or building in which books are kept for reading.
Public **libraries** lend books.

lick

Pussy likes to **lick** her fur.
She runs her tongue over it.

lid

The pan has a **lid**.
It has a cover over it.

lie, lying, lay, lain

Dad wished to **lie** down.
He wished to stretch out flat.
He is **lying** on the couch.
He **lay** down after dinner.
He has **lain** there all evening.

lieutenant

A **lieutenant** is an officer in the army or navy.

life

A turtle's **life** is long.
It lives many years.

lift

Martin cannot **lift** the box. He cannot raise it from the floor.

light

1. Tom will **light** the fire.
He will start it burning.
2. When we have **light**, we can see easily.
The sun gives **light**.
A lamp gives **light**.

Dad turned on the **light**.
3. Feathers are **light**.
They do not weigh much.
4. The apron is **light** blue.
It is pale blue.

lightning

Lightning is electricity.
We see it in the sky during a thunder storm.

like

1. Jayne's hat looks **like** Mary's. The girls have the same kind of hat.
2. The children **like** the story.
The story pleases them.

likely

Grace is **likely** to win the game. It looks as though she is going to win.

lilac

A **lilac** bush has purple or white flowers.

lily, lilies

A **lily** is a plant.
A **lily** is the flower of the plant. Two **lilies** are blooming on this plant.

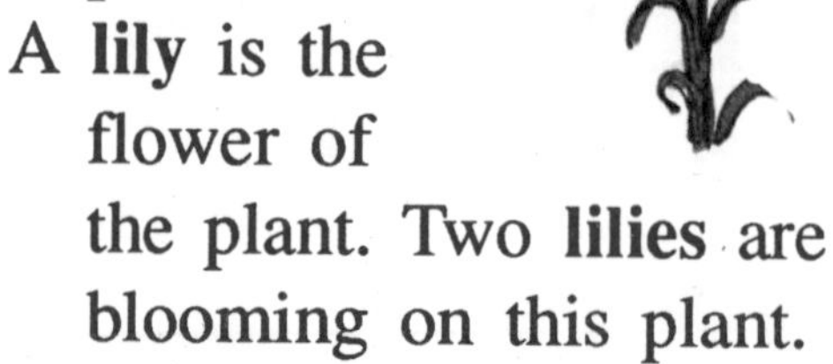

limb

1. A branch of a tree is called a **limb**.
2. A leg, an arm, or a wing is called a **limb**.

lime

1. A **lime** is a green fruit.
2. **Lime** is a white powder made from a kind of stone.

limit

We passed the city **limit**.
It was the edge of the city.

line, lines

1. We stood in **line**.
We stood one after the other.
2. The paper has **lines**.
It has straight marks.

linen

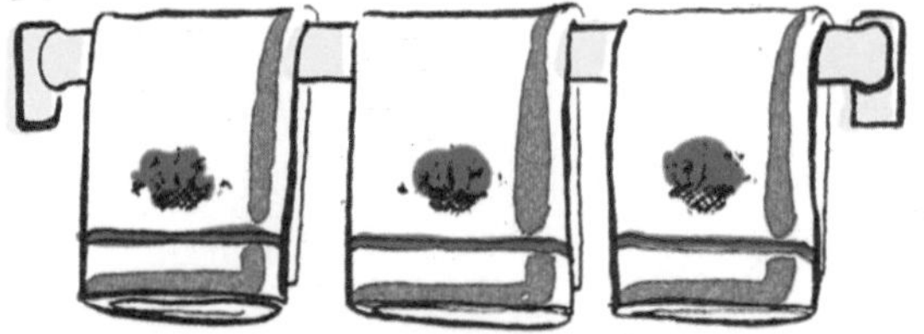

These are **linen** towels.
Linen is a cloth.
It is made from flax.

lion

A **lion** is a wild beast.
It has a mane.

lip

A **lip** is the edge of the mouth.
The mouth has an upper **lip** and a lower **lip**.

liquid

A **liquid** is wet.
It can be poured.
Water is a **liquid**.
Milk is a **liquid**.

list

I have a **list** of things to buy at the store.
I have a number of things written on the **list**.

listen

We **listen** with our ears.
We **listen** to music.
We hear the music.

little

Fluffy is a **little** dog.
Fluffy is small in size.

live

I **live** in a city.
My home is in the city.

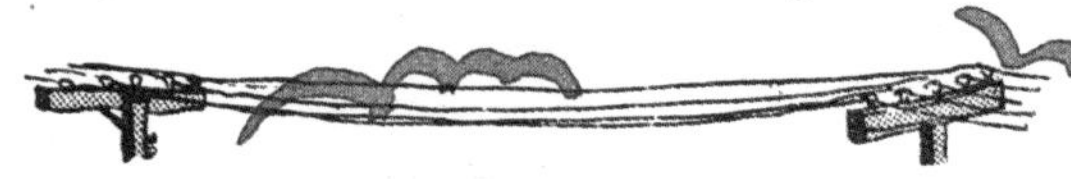

This is a **live** wire.
It carries electric current.

lively

Tennis is a **lively** game.
The players move quickly.

load

1. The men **load** the truck with furniture and boxes.
They put things into the truck.
2. The truck carries a large **load**. The truck can hold a large amount of goods.

loaf, loaves

A **loaf** is a portion of bread.
Here are two **loaves** of bread.

local

1. This is a **local** train.
It stops at every station.
2. The hero is a **local** man.
He comes from this city.

lock, locked

1. We **lock** the door with a key. Then the door cannot be opened without the key.
2. The trunk has a **lock**.

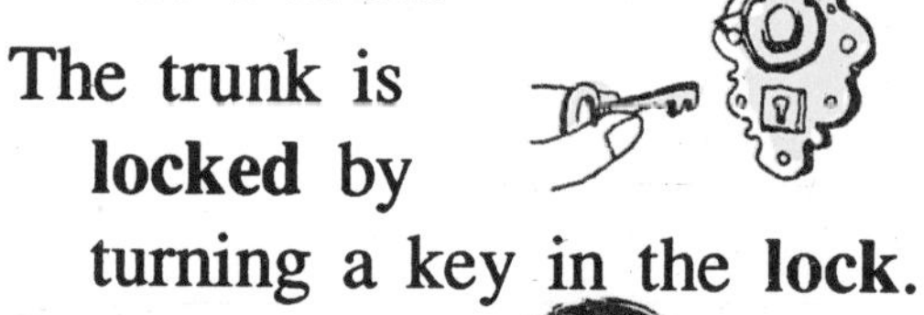

The trunk is **locked** by turning a key in the **lock**.
3. Anna cut off a **lock** of hair.
She cut off several hairs.

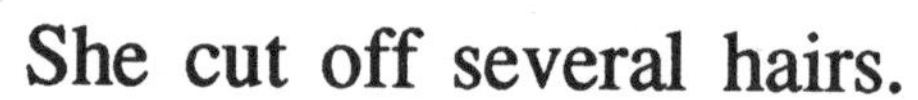

locker

At school I hang my coat in a **locker**.
It is a cupboard with a **lock**.

L
M
N
O
P
Q
R
S
T
U
V
W
X
Y
Z

love, lovely

We **love** our mother.
She is very dear to us.
She is **lovely**.
She is sweet and beautiful.

low

1. The bridge is **low**.
It is not high.
2. The light is **low**.
It is not bright.
3. Rose's voice is **low**.
It is not loud.

luck, lucky

I had **luck** today.
This was my **lucky** day.
Good things happened all day.

lump

This is a **lump** of sugar.
It is a piece of sugar.

lunch

Lunch is a light meal,
usually eaten at noon.

lung, lungs

A **lung** is part of the body.
Two **lungs** are in the chest.
We breathe with **lungs.**

M m

Ma, Mama, Mamma

These are names for mother.

machine, machines

A **machine** has parts which move to do some work.
These are **machines**.

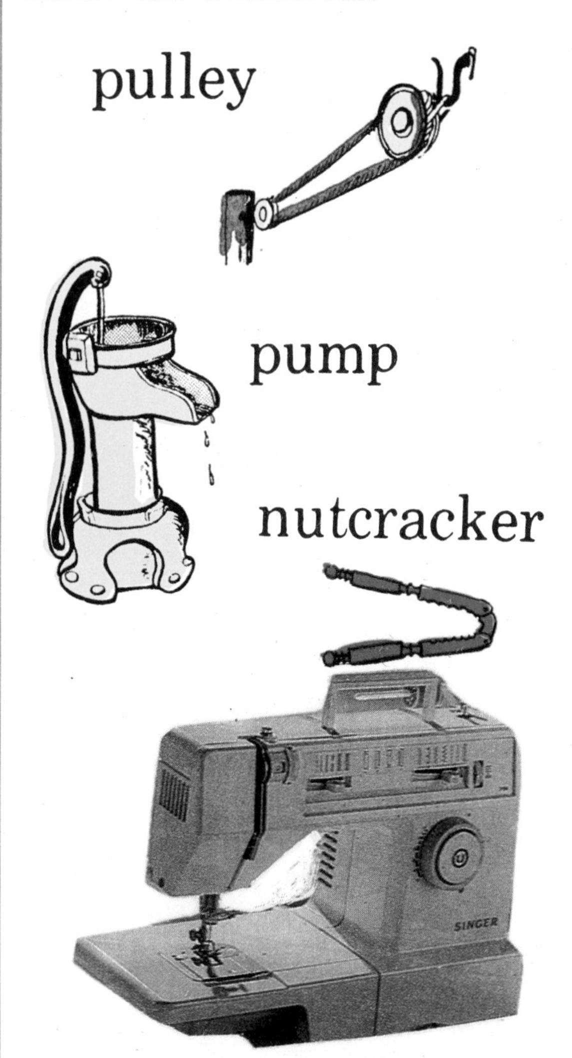

make, making, made

Laura can **make** a cake.

Tom is **making** a model plane.

Rose has **made** a dress.
We put materials together
when we **make** something.

man, men

Daddy
is a
man.

The **men** are mending the
road.

manage

1. When Mother is sick, I
manage to get breakfast.
I do the best that I can.
2. Two men **manage** the office.
They are in charge of it.

mane

The horse
has long, thick hair on
its neck. It is a **mane**.

manner, manners

1. Let us work in this
manner.
Let us work in this way.
2. Don has good **manners**.
Don is polite.

mansion

A **mansion** is a large house.

manual

1. Carpentry is **manual** work.
It is done with the hands.
2. The game has a **manual**.
It has a book that tells
how to play the game.

manufacture

We **manufacture** cars here.
We make cars here.

marriage, married

The **marriage** of my sister took place in church.
Andrew and Rose were **married**.
Now they live together as husband and wife.

mask

A **mask** is a false face.
It is usually made of cloth.
It fits over the face.

mass

1. A **mass** of material is a great amount of material.
2. A **mass** of people is a great number of people.
3. A **Mass** is a church service.

mast, masts

A **mast** is an upright pole.
It holds a sail.
The ship has three **masts**.

master

1. The dog belongs to Tom.
Tom is its **master**.
2. We must **master** the lesson.
We must learn the lesson.

mat

1. A **mat** is a small rug.
We put a **mat** on the floor.
2. A **mat** is a bit of cloth.
We put a **mat** on the table.

match, matches

1. A **match** is a small stick.
The head of a **match** will burn when it is scratched.
It is dangerous to play with **matches**.
2. The two colours **match**.
They are exactly alike.
3. We had a swimming **match**.
We had swimming races.

mate

A **mate** is one of a pair.
The bird is red.
His **mate** is green.

material

A **material** is anything that we use in making something.
Cloth is **material** for clothes.
Metal is **material** for tools.
Wood is **material** for chairs.

matter

1. What is the **matter** with Ann?
   What is wrong with Ann?
2. The election of officers is an important **matter**.
It is an important thing.

mattress

A **mattress** is a long, flat cushion that fits on a bed.

may

1. Mother says that I **may** go.
Mother will allow me to go.
2. We **may** go away.
It is possible that we shall go away.

maybe

Maybe the rain will stop.
Perhaps it will stop.

mayor

A **mayor** is the head of a city government.

me

Tom said, "Give **me** the book."
I gave the book to Tom.

meadow

A **meadow** is a grassy field.

meal, meals

1. A **meal** is the food eaten at a regular time.
Breakfast is a **meal**.
Lunch and dinner are **meals**.
2. **Meal** is powdered grain.
Corn is ground into **meal**.

mean, meaning, meant

What does the word **mean**?
What idea does it express?
The dictionary explains the **meaning** of words.
I found what the word **meant**.
Now I understand the word.

M N O P Q R S T U V W X Y Z

means

1. Our club has small **means**.
Our club has little money.
2. We found **means** of earning money.
We found ways.

measles

Measles is a disease.

measure

1. The man will **measure** my foot. He will find its size.
2. A **measure** is used to find the size or amount of a thing.
This **measure** holds a cupful of anything.

meat

Meat is a food.
Meat is the flesh of animals.

medicine

I took **medicine** when I was ill.
Medicine made me feel better.

medal

Uncle Tom has a **medal**.
He won it because he was brave.

medium

The cloth has **medium** quality.
It has not the best nor the worst quality.

meet, meeting, met

Our club will **meet** today.
The members will gather today.
Our **meeting** is on Tuesday.
We **met** last Tuesday.

melon

A **melon** is a round fruit.
It grows on a vine.

melt

The ice has begun to **melt**.
Heat turns it into water.

member

Ann is a **member** of the club.
Ann belongs to the club.

memory, memories

Grandma's **memory** is good.
She can call things to mind.
She has happy **memories**.
She remembers things that she did long ago.

M N O P Q R S T U V W X Y Z

meter

A gas **meter** measures the amount of gas that we use.
A parking **meter** measures the time that the car is parked.

method

This is the robin's **method** of getting food.
This is its way of doing it.

middle

Ted's arrow hit the **middle** of the target.
The **middle** is at an equal distance from all sides.

midnight

Midnight is twelve o'clock at night.

might

I **might** have a party.
It is possible.

mighty

The athlete is **mighty**.
He is large and strong.

mild

1. I had a **mild** attack of measles.
I was not very ill.
2. The weather is **mild**.
It is not cold.

mile

A **mile** is a measure of distance.
I can walk a **mile** in about fifteen minutes.

milk, milkman

Milk is a liquid food.
We get it from a cow.
The **milkman** brings milk every day.

mill, miller

A **mill** grinds grain into meal or flour.
A **miller** works in a mill.

million 1,000,000

A **million** is a very big number.

miss, misses

1. Rose used to be **Miss** Hopkins. She is married now. She is Mrs. Clark.
2. I saw Dad **miss** a train.
He did not catch the train.
When he **misses** that train, he is late for work.

mist

There is **mist** in the air.
There is water in the air.
It is finer than rain.

mistake

There is a **mistake** in my work.
My work is not right.

mistress

The cat belongs to Jane.
She is its **mistress**.

mitten

A **mitten** is worn on the hand.
It is a glove with one part for the fingers and a smaller part for the thumb.

mix, mixture

We **mix** flour and other things to make cake.
We put them together.
The **mixture** is called batter.

mock

1. We had a **mock** wedding.
We had a make-believe wedding.
2. It is unkind to **mock** anyone. It is unkind to make fun of anyone.

model

Tom made a **model**. It is a small copy of an aeroplane.

modern

This is a **modern** house.
It is new and up-to-date.

mosquito

A **mosquito** is an insect.
We hear it buzz.
It bites people.

moss

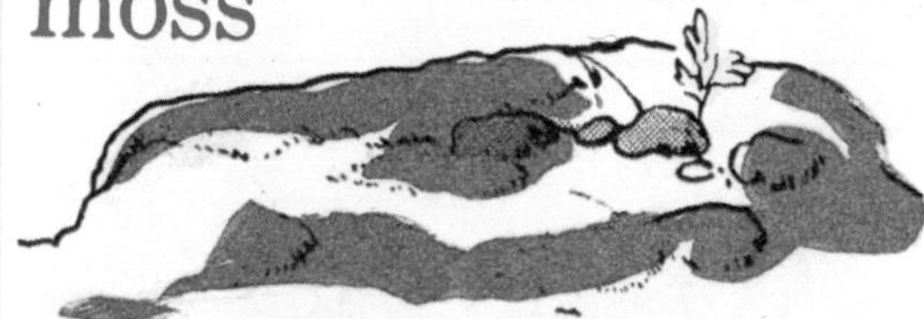

Moss is growing on the rock.
It is a soft, green plant.
It has no flowers.

most

We had a peanut hunt.
Dick found the **most** peanuts.
He found the largest number.

moth

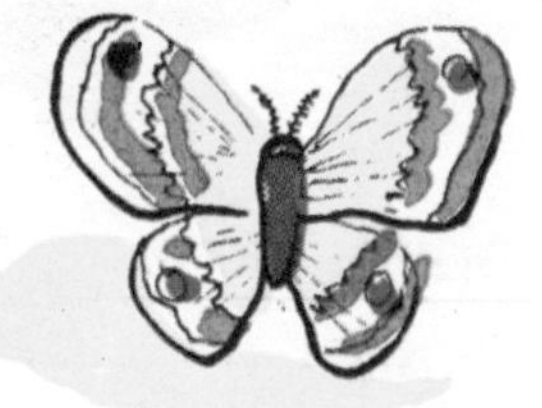

A **moth** is an
insect with
wings.
This is a **moth**.

mother

My **mother** has six children.
Puss is a **mother**, too.
She has five kittens.

motion

The car is in **motion**.
It is moving.

motor

A **motor** is a machine that
causes motion.
A **motor** makes the car go.

mount

1. Ted will **mount** the horse.
He will get on the horse.
2. I shall **mount** the picture.
I shall paste it on cardboard.

mountain

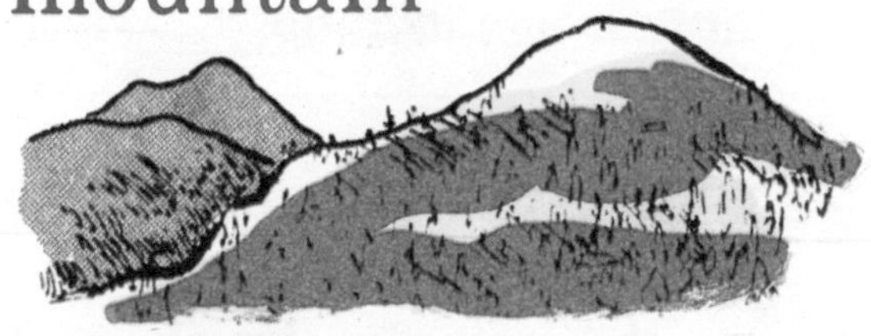

A **mountain** is very high
land.
It is higher than a hill.

mouse, mice

A **mouse** is a small animal.
Mice like to eat cheese.

mouth

The **mouth** is
part of the face.
It is used for eating
and talking.

move

Nicola is going to **move**.
She will live in another house.
Two men **move** the piano.
Two men take the piano
from one place to another.

moving picture

A **moving picture** is a
series of pictures that
are thrown on a screen.
They change so quickly
that people and things
in the picture seem to
be moving.

mow

Tom has to **mow** the lawn.
He has to cut the grass.

much

We have not **much** bread.
We have not a large amount.

mud, muddy

Judy is making **mud** pies
out of water and dirt.
Her hands are **muddy**.
They are covered with **mud**.

muff

A **muff** is a
covering to
keep the hands warm.

mule

A **mule** is an animal.
A **mule** used to do work
on the farm.

multiply, multiplication

1. Germs **multiply**. They
grow greater in number.
2. In arithmetic we **multiply**.
7 times 7 are 49.
That is **multiplication**.

museum

A **museum** is a building
where valuable things
are kept for people to see.
We visited a **museum** of art.
We saw examples of great art.

music, musician

Music is pleasing to hear.
People sing **music**.
People play **music** on
many instruments.
A **musician** is one who writes,
sings, or plays **music**.

must

I **must** sweep the path.
I should sweep the path.

mustard

Mustard is a hot, spicy paste.
We use **mustard** on our food to
bring out the taste.

my

Paul says,
"This is **my** sled.
It belongs to me."
The sled belongs to Paul.

myself

I painted the cart **myself**.
I did the work all alone.

N n

nail

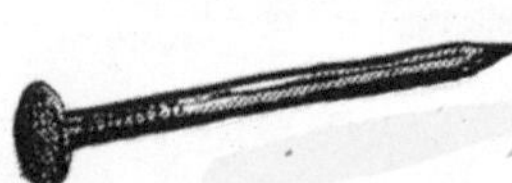

A **nail** is a piece of metal.
It has a flat head.
It has a sharp point.
A **nail** fastens together
pieces of wood.

name, names

Every person has a **name**.
My sister's **name** is Ann.
Everything has a **name**.

cart

drum

Places have **names**.
Denver is the **name** of a city.

M N O P Q R S T U V W X Y Z

nap

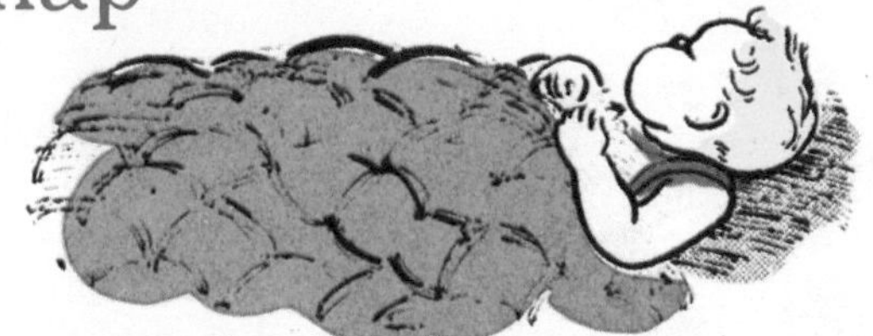

Baby takes a **nap**.
He sleeps for a short time.

napkin

A **napkin** is a
piece of cloth or paper.
It is used during a meal to
keep lips and hands clean.

narrow

The path is **narrow**. It is
not far from side to side.

nasturtium

A **nasturtium** is a flower.
It has a bright colour.

nation

A **nation** is a country.
Its people usually have the
same language, history,
and government.

national

July 4th is a **national** holiday
in the United States.
It is a holiday for all the
nation.

native

I am a **native** of England.
I was born in England.

nature, natural

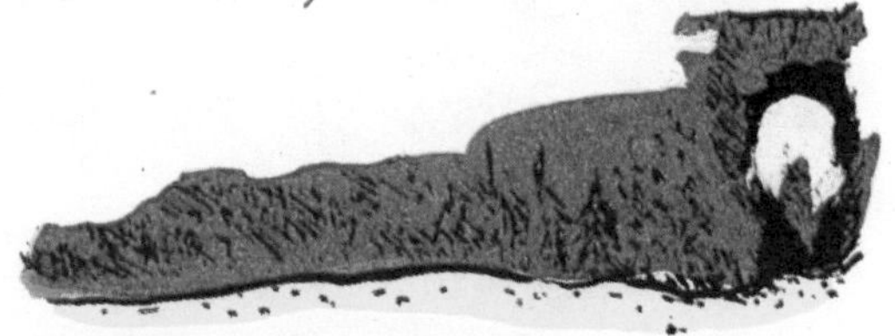

Things in **nature** are
things not made by man.
The **Natural** Bridge was
made by **nature**.

naughty, naughtier, naughtiest

Judy was **naughty** today.
She behaved badly.
When she was punished,
she became **naughtier**.
The **naughtiest** thing that she
did was to tease the baby.

navy, navies

Our country has a **navy**.
We have ships and men
that fight for us in time
of war.
Navies fight on the sea
and in the air.

near, nearer, nearest

I live **near** the school.
I live not far from school.
Ben lives **nearer**. Dick
lives **nearest**. He lives
next door to the school.

neither

Neither Dora nor I may go.
We must both stay at home.

nephew

Rose is my sister.
Rose has a son.
He is my **nephew**.

nervous

Anna has to say a poem.
She is **nervous**.
She is afraid that she will make a mistake.

nest

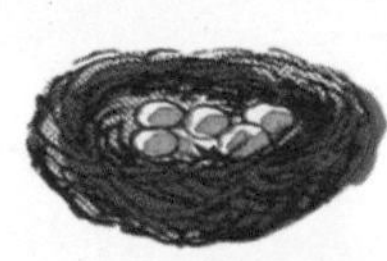

Robins built a **nest** in the apple tree. It is their home. There are five blue eggs in the **nest**.

net

A **net** is open material made of knotted threads.

Men catch fish in a **net**.
The tennis court has a **net**.
Rose wears a **net** on her hair.

never

Peter Pan **never** grew up.
He was always a little boy.

new

Jane has a **new** coat.
She bought it last week.
This is the first time that she has worn it.

news

We hear **news** on the radio.
We read it in the newspaper.
We see **news** on the television.
We learn about things that happen in the world.

newspaper, newspapers

News is printed in the **newspaper**. There are several pages of news.
Most **newspapers** are printed every day.

N
O
P
Q
R
S
T
U
V
W
X
Y
Z

no

1. Dorothy has **no** money.
Her purse is empty.
2. Did you see the parade?
No, I did not see it.

noble, nobleman

1. The boy is of **noble** birth.
His father is a **nobleman**.
The rank of **nobleman**
is given by a king.
2. Men faced danger to
save the wounded soldiers.
It was a **noble** thing to do.
It was a great thing to do.

nobody

We are selling lemonade.
Nobody has come to buy.
No person has come to buy.

nod

Ask Baby if he wants a biscuit.
He will **nod** his head.
He will move his
head up and down.

noise, noisy, noisier, noisiest

Our band makes **noise**.
It makes a loud sound.
Judy's horn is **noisy**.
Ben's drum is **noisier**.
Sam has a pan and spoon.
That is the **noisiest** of all.

none

Andrew would like some
chocolate.
There is **none** left.
There is not any chocolate left.

noon, noonday

Noon is the middle of the day.
The **noonday** sun is overhead.

nor

Neither Paul **nor** Donald
can reach the apple.
Paul cannot reach it, and
Donald cannot reach it.

nurse

1. A **nurse** takes care of little children.
2. A **nurse** takes care of people who are sick.

nut, nuts, nutcracker

1. A **nut** has a hard shell.
These are **nuts**.
We break the shell with a **nutcracker**.
We eat the kernel inside.
2. A **nut** is a piece of metal.
It holds a screw or rod in place.

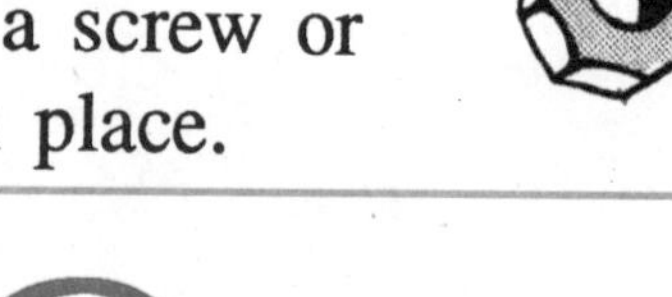

O o

oak

This **oak** tree is old.
Acorns grow on **oak** trees.

oar, oars

An **oar** is made of wood.
It has a blade and a long handle. A boat is rowed with two **oars**.

oats, oatmeal

Oats are the seeds of a grain.
Horses eat **oats**.
We eat **oatmeal** made from **oats**.

obey

We should **obey** our parents and teachers.
We should do as they say.

object

An **object** is a thing.
We are learning how to draw a square **object**.

object

We do not play on the lawn
Father would **object**.
He would not like it.

oblige

Billy will **oblige** us by
singing songs that we like.
He will please us.

oblong

An **oblong** has four sides.
Two sides are longer than
the other two sides.

observe

Observe the picture.
Look at it carefully.

obtain

We **obtain** milk at school.
We get milk at school.

occupy, occupying, occupied

People came to **occupy**
the big red house.
They came to live there.
Two families are **occupying** it.
It had not been **occupied**
for several months.

occur

Where did the fire **occur**?
Where did it happen?

ocean, oceans

The **ocean** is a large
area of salt water.
There are five **oceans:**
Atlantic **Ocean**
Indian **Ocean**
Pacific **Ocean**
Arctic **Ocean**
Antarctic **Ocean**

o'clock

It is seven **o'clock.**
It is seven by the clock.

odd

1. **Odd** numbers cannot
be divided exactly by two.
These are **odd** numbers:
1 3 5 7 9
2. That is an **odd** hat.
It is an unusual hat.
3. Henry does **odd** jobs.
He does different jobs.

odour

The turkey is roasting.
It has a pleasant odour.
It has a pleasant smell.

of

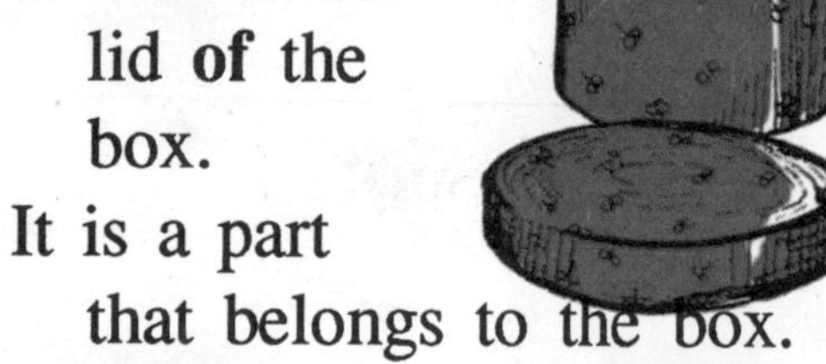

1. This is the lid **of** the box.
It is a part that belongs to the box.
2. The table is made **of** wood.
Wood was used to make it.
3. I like stories **of** animals.
I like stories about animals.
4. Billy is six years **of** age.
Billy is six years old.
5. One **of** the eggs is cracked.
One egg among the others is cracked.

off

Spot knocked the lamp **off** the hall table.
The lamp was on the table.
Now it is on the floor.

offend

Do not laugh at Brian
You would **offend** him.
You would hurt his feelings.

offer

Mother told me to **offer** Mary some chocolate.
She told me to pass Mary the chocolate.

office

1. An **office** is a room where business is carried on.
Daddy has an **office** where he does his business.
2. The Queen has an **office** at Buckingham Place.

officer, officers

An **officer** wears a uniform.
A policeman is an **officer**.
The Army, the Navy, and the Marines have **officers**.
They are in charge of men.

often

I wash my hands **often.**
I wash them many times.

O P Q R S T U V W X Y Z

only

1. Mary is an **only** child.
She has no brothers
and no sisters.
2. We had **only** soup to eat.
We had soup and nothing else.

open

1. The door is **open.**
It is not shut.
2. Harry will **open** his
lunch box at noon.
He will take off the cover.

opening

We made a small **opening**
in the bird house.
We made a small hole, so
that the bird could go
into the house.

opera

An **opera** is a play.
The words are not spoken.
The words are sung.
An orchestra plays the music.

operation

Donald had an **operation**.
The doctor had to cut out
Donald's tonsils.

opinion

Edward's **opinion** is that
the hay should be cut.
That is what he thinks.

opportunity, opportunities

An **opportunity** is a chance
to do something good.
Jim had two **opportunities**
to work last summer.

opposite

1. Don is **opposite** Dot.
Don is facing Dot.
2. Hot is **opposite** to cold.
Thin is **opposite** to fat.

or

We may have chocolate
or vanilla ice cream.
We may choose one
of two flavours.

orange

An **orange** is a fruit.
Orange trees grow
in warm countries.

orchard

There are many fruit trees
in Uncle Henry's **orchard**.

orchestra

An **orchestra** plays music.
An **orchestra** has several
players and instruments.

order

1. The major gave an **order**.
He told his men what to do.
2. The books are in **order**.
Each book is in its place.
3. Our class is in **order**.
We are behaving well.

organ

1. An **organ** is an
instrument for making
music.
Mr. Bly plays the **organ**.
2. An **organ** of the body
does special work.
The stomach is an **organ**.
The stomach digests food.

organize

We **organize** our class.
We have officers and
several committees to do
our work.

original

Jayne's drawing is **original**.
The idea is her own.
It was not copied.

oriole

The **oriole**
is a bird.
It has an orange breast.
Its nest is a little basket.

outside

Spot is **outside** the door.
He would like to come in.

oven

An **oven**
is part of a stove used
for baking and roasting.
Mother put the cake into
the **oven** to bake.

over

1. At night
we put a cloth
over the parrot's cage.
We cover it with a cloth.
2. Holiday is **over.**
Holiday has ended.

overalls

Overalls are clothing
used for work or play.
Peter wears **overalls** when
he works in the garden.

overcoat

It is cold.
Dad wears
his
overcoat.
It is a long, warm coat
to be worn outdoors.

owe

We **owe** Tom some money.
He loaned us some money.
We should pay him back.

owl

The **owl** is a
night bird.
It has big,
round eyes.

own, owner

1. That is John's **own**
bicycle. It is his.
He is the **owner** of it.

ox, oxen

An **ox** is a large animal.
In olden days **oxen**
pulled heavy loads.

P p

pa, papa

Pa and **Papa** are short
names for Father.

pack

1. The donkey carries a
pack on its back.
It carries a bundle.
2. Wolves go in a **pack.**
Many wolves go together.
3. This is a
pack of
cards.

4. Mother will **pack** our
trunk when we go away.
She will put our
clothes into the trunk.

package

The shoes are in a **package.**
They are wrapped up
for us to carry.

pad, pads

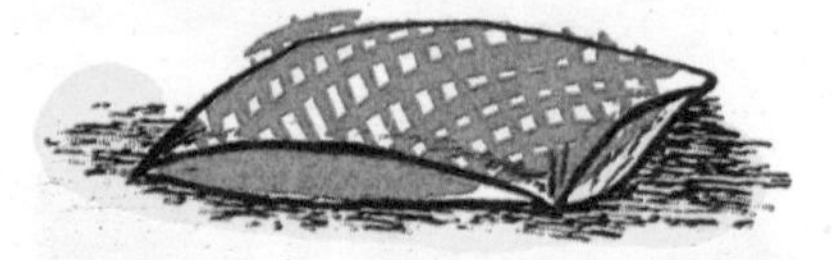

1. A **pad** is a cushion.
2. This is
a **pad** of
paper.
3. A dog has
pads on its
feet.

paddle

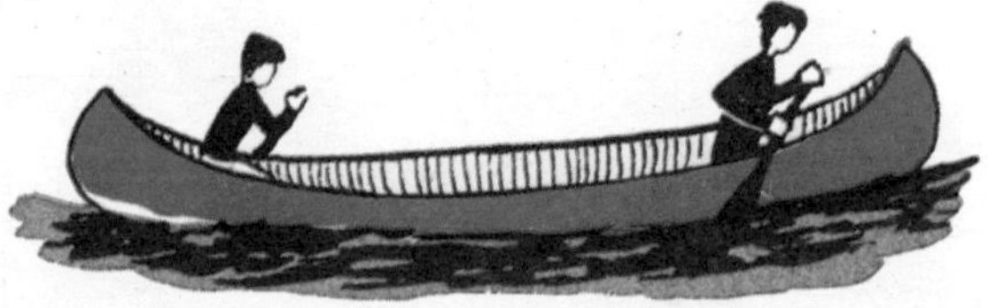

The boys **paddle** the canoe.
They send it through the
water.
A **paddle** is like an oar.
Each boy has a **paddle.**

page

A **page** is one side of a
leaf of paper in a book.
A picture is on this **page.**

P Q R S T U V W X Y Z

pancake

A **pancake** is a thin, flat cake.
It is cooked in a pan.

pane

A **pane** is a piece of glass.
It is part of a window.

pansy, pansies

Dot picked a purple **pansy** and a yellow **pansy**.
Pansies are pretty flowers.

pants

1. **Pants** are clothing worn on the legs.
Charles has short **pants**.
Pat has long **pants**.
2. The dog **pants**.
He takes short, quick breaths.

paper

Paper is made from wood, cloth, or old **paper**.
We write on **paper**.
We have **paper** cups.

parachute

The man jumped from a plane.
He has a **parachute**.
It will carry him to earth.

parade

We saw a circus **parade**.
It came down the street.

parasol

Aunt Jackie has a **parasol**.
It is an umbrella.
It shades her from the sun.

parcel, parcel post

Grace has a **parcel**.
It is wrapped in paper and tied, to be sent by mail.
It will go by **parcel post**.

partner

1. Russell is Virginia's **partner** in the dance.
Russell dances with Virginia.
2. Dad has a **partner**.
He and his **partner** own a business.

party, parties

Trudy had a **party**.
She invited her friends.
They played games.
They had something to eat.
Parties are fun.

pass

1. Tony will **pass** Harry.
He will run ahead of Harry.
2. Please **pass** the butter.
Please hand me the butter.
3. Louis took a test.
He hopes to **pass** well.
He hopes to get a good mark.

passenger

Kate is a **passenger** on a bus.
She is riding on a bus.

past

1. The fire engine went **past**.
It went by.
2. In the **past**, Grandfather had a large farm.
He had it in years gone by.

paste

Mary has a jar of **paste**.
She uses it to **paste** pictures in her book.
It makes the pictures stick to the pages of the book.

pasteboard

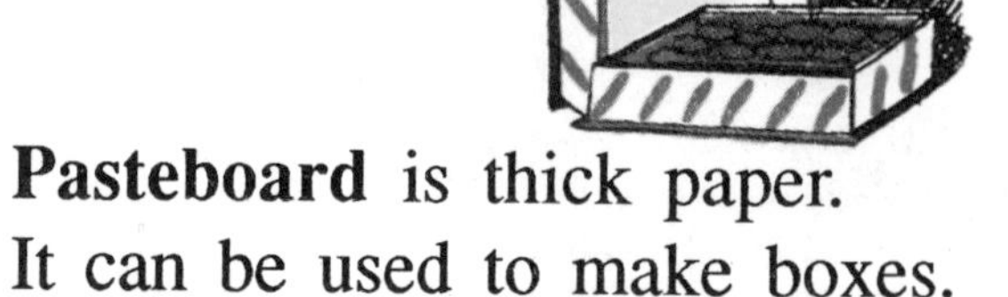

Pasteboard is thick paper.
It can be used to make boxes.

peas

Peas are a green vegetable.

peace

The war is over.
Fighting has stopped.
We have **peace**.

peach, peaches

A **peach** is a fruit.
Peaches have soft skins.

peanut, peanuts

A **peanut** is a nut.
Peanuts grow on a plant.
The nuts grow underground.

pear

A **pear** is a fruit.
It is juicy.

pearl

A **pearl** is used as a jewel.
It is found in an oyster.

peck

Hens **peck** at food.
They take a little food at a time with their beaks.

peel

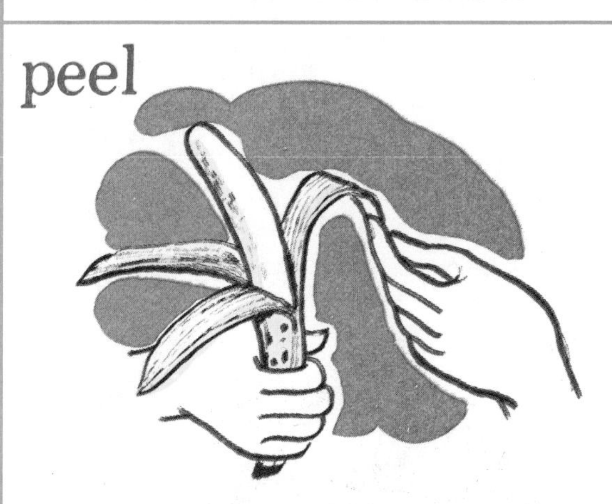

A banana has a **peel**.
It has a thick skin.
We **peel** the banana.
We take off the skin.

peep

1. **Peep** into the room.
Open the door a little, and look into the room.
2. Baby chicks **peep**.
They make a shrill sound.

peg

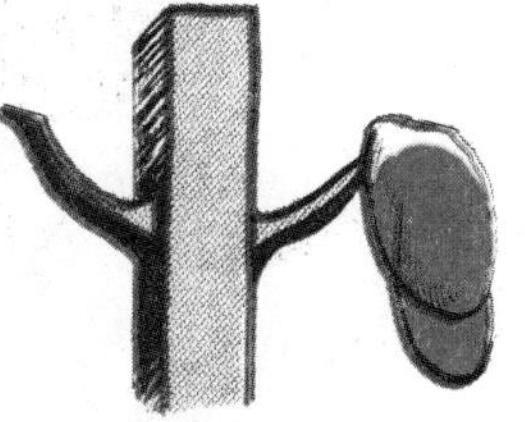

A **peg** is a pin of wood or metal.
The cap hangs on a **peg**.

period

1. A **period** is a dot.
A **period** is put at the end of a written statement.
2. A **period** is a length of time. The art **period** is forty minutes long.

permission, permit

Ann has **permission** to go.
Mother says that she may go.
Mother will **permit** her to go.

person

A **person** is a man or a woman or a child.

pet

A **pet** is an animal that we keep to play with.
Mary had a **pet** lamb.

petal

A **petal** is part of a flower.
A **petal** dropped from the rose.

petroleum

Petroleum is a thick oil.
It comes from the ground.
Petroleum will burn.
It is used for light, for heat, and for power.
Dye, medicine, and other things are made from it.

petticoat

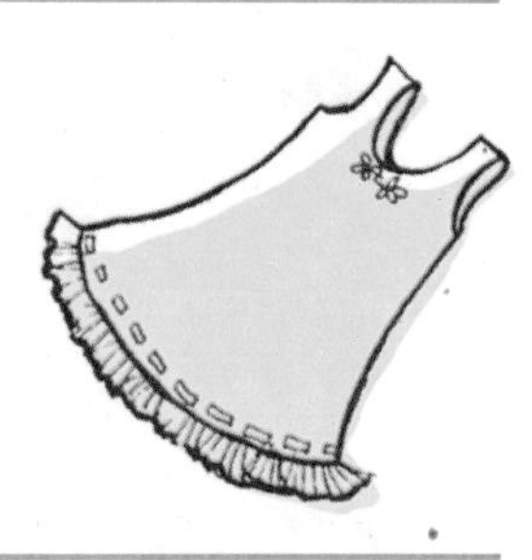

A **petticoat** is a skirt worn under a dress.

photograph

A **photograph** is a picture.
It is made with a camera.

piano

A **piano** is an instrument for making music.

P Q R S T U V W X Y Z

pick

1. Terry will **pick** apples.
He will take the apples
from the apple tree.

2. A **pick** is a tool.
The man uses a **pick** to
break the hard road.
3. We are trying to **pick**
the kind of sweets we like.
We are trying to choose.

pickle

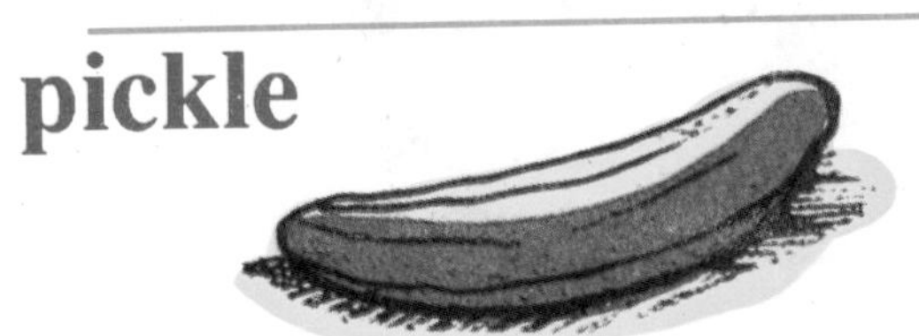

A **pickle** is a vegetable or
fruit. It has been kept
in salt and vinegar.

picnic

A **picnic**
is a meal eaten outdoors.
We have fun at a **picnic.**

picture

Jayne
drew a **picture** of a house.

pie

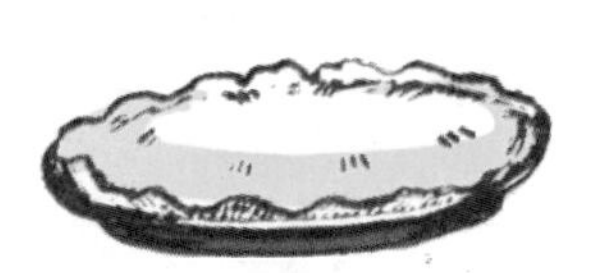

A **pie** is food.
It is made of fruit
or other material.
It is baked in a
paste made of flour.

piece

Mother cut a
piece from
the pie.
She cut a part
from the pie.

pig

A **pig** is a farm animal.
This **pig** is fat.

pint

The milkman left a
quart and a **pint** of milk.
A **pint** is half a quart.

pipe

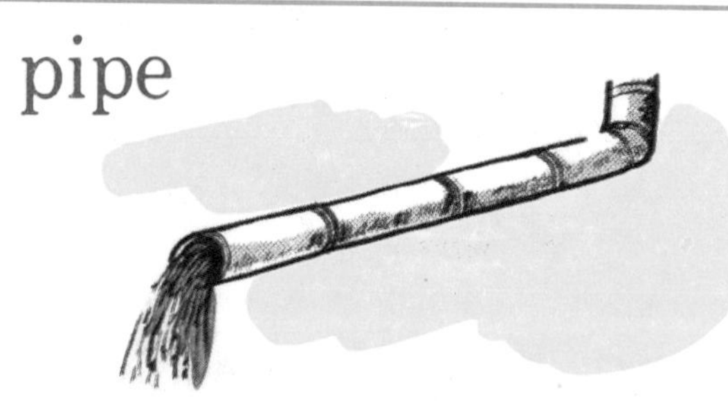

1. A **pipe** is a hollow tube.
Water runs through the **pipe**.

2. Father smokes a **pipe**.
He burns tobacco in his **pipe**.

pistol

A **pistol** is a small weapon.
It can be held in the hand.
It fires a bullet.

pit

1. A **pit**
is a hole in the earth.
2. The peach
has a **pit**.

It is a seed inside the peach.

pitch

1. Pat will **pitch**.
He will throw the ball.
2. **Pitch** is a black
and sticky material.

pitcher

1. The
pitcher throws the ball.

2. A **pitcher** is a dish.
It is used to hold a liquid.
Milk is in the **pitcher**.

pity

I **pity** the birds on cold days.
I feel sorry for them.

play

1. A **play** is a story acted on the stage. We wrote a **play** about Cinderella.
2. We **play** games for fun.
3. Grace can **play** the violin. She can make music on it.

playmate

Jayne is Ann's **playmate**.
They play together.

pleasant

Mandy has a **pleasant** smile.
Her smile gives us pleasure.

please, pleasure

1. The gift will **please** Dad. It will give him **pleasure**. He will like it.
2. We cannot always do as we **please**. We cannot always do as we like.

plenty

Terry has **plenty** of apples.
He has a great many.

plough, ploughs

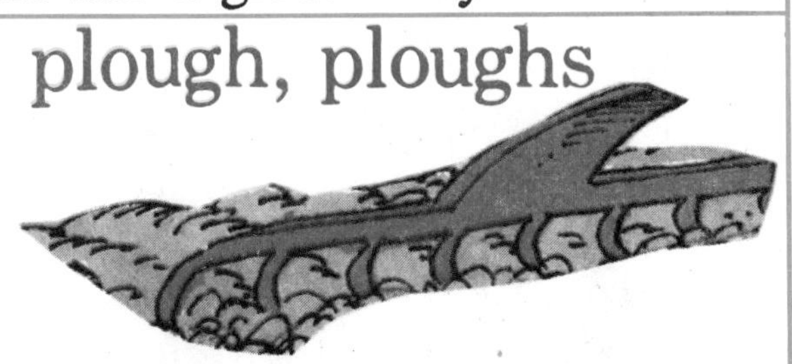

A **plough** is a tool used on the farm.
A **plough** turns over the ground.
Uncle Henry **ploughs** in spring.

plum

A **plum** is a fruit.
It has a smooth skin.

pocket

A **pocket** is a bag made in clothing.
Jennie's apron has a **pocket**.

pocketbook

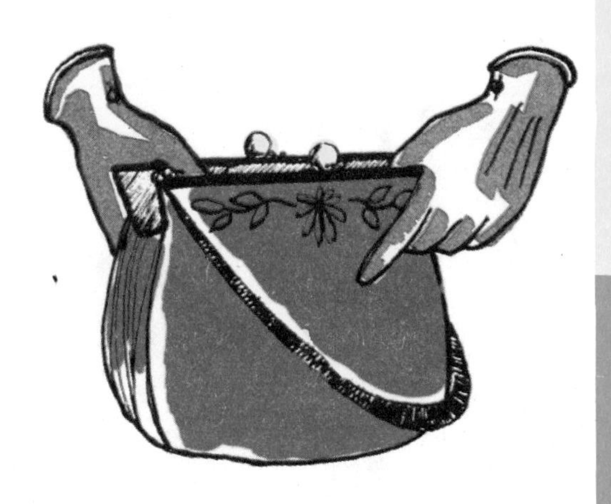

Anna has a red **pocketbook**.
It is a small bag used for carrying money.

poem, poet

A **poem** is writing in verse.
It expresses deep feeling.
Its words are like music.
A **poem** is written by a **poet**.

point

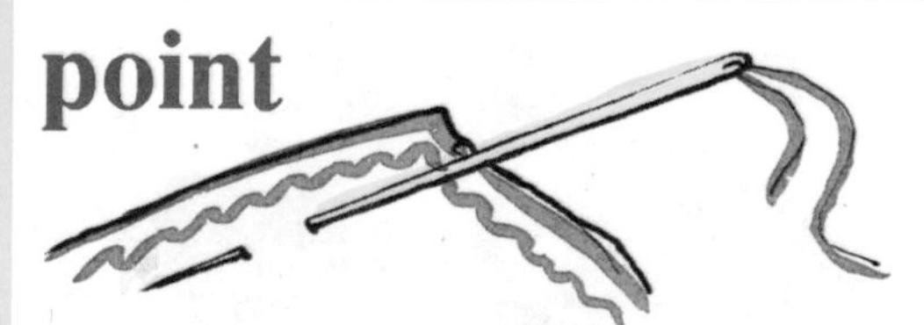

A needle has a sharp **point**.
It is sharp at one end.

poison

Poison must not be eaten.
It causes sickness or death.

poke

We **poke**
the fire with a stick.
We push it to make it burn.

pole

The **pole** holds the wires.
A **pole** is a long stick.

policeman

A **policeman** is a person
who keeps order in
public places.

polish

We **polish** the silver.
We rub it to make it shine.

polite

John is **polite**. He is kind.
He has good manners.

pond

Ben sails
his boat on the **pond**.
A **pond** is a stretch of water.
It is smaller than a lake.

pony, ponies

A **pony** is a small horse.
They have **ponies** at the park.

present

1. All the boys and girls
   in class are **present**.
All of them are here.
2. Jane has a **present**.
It is a gift from Grace.

present

1. We shall **present** a play.
We shall act in the play
   before an audience.
2. Jim will **present**
   our gift to the teacher.
He will give her the gift.

president

A **president** is elected
   by a group of people
   to be their leader.
Many countries elect
   a **president** as ruler.

press

Rose had to **press** a dress.
She took out the wrinkles by
   smoothing it with an iron.

pretend

We **pretend**
   that the chairs are a train.
We play that they are a
   train.

pretty, prettier, prettiest

All the tulips are **pretty**.
They are pleasing to see.
Do you think that the
   yellow ones are **prettier**
   than the others?
Which is **prettiest**?

prevent

Try to **prevent** accidents.
Try to be careful, so that
   accidents do not happen.

price

What is the **price** of the cap?
How much does it cost?

prick

Thorns can **prick** the finger.
They stick into the finger.

pride, proud

Bob has **pride** in his work.
He likes to do it well.
He is **proud** of his record.
He is pleased, because
his work is good.

priest

A **priest** is a man trained
in the work of religion.

prince, princess

A **prince** is the son
of a king and queen.
A **princess** is the daughter
of a king and queen,
or the wife of a prince.

principal

1. Our school is the
principal school in the
city.
It is the largest and best.

2. Mr. Hayes is **principal**.
He is the head of the
school.

principle

A **principle** is a rule.
It is a good **principle**
always to be honest.

print, printer

1. We **print** with type.
Type is covered with ink,
and pressed on the
paper.
The work is done by a
printer.
2. This book has large
print.
It has large letters.

prison, prisoner

People who break the law
are often kept in a
prison.
A **prisoner** lives in a **prison**.

private

Our yard is **private**.
It is used only by our family.

prize

Russell won a **prize**.
He won a reward for good
work.

P Q R S T U V W X Y Z

property

Mr. Jones owns **property**.
He owns a house and land.

protect

Prince will **protect** Baby.
He will let nothing harm
Baby.

protection

Ruth's
raincoat
gives her
protection
from the
rain.
It keeps her from getting wet.

prove

Can you **prove** that
your answer is right?
Can you show that
it is surely right?

provide

The teacher will **provide**
ice cream for our party.
She will give the ice cream.

prune

A **prune** is a dried plum.

public

The post office is a
public building.
It is used by all people.

pudding

Pudding is a dessert.
It is boiled or baked.

puddle

Donald has new boots.
He steps in every **puddle**.
A **puddle** is a small hollow
place filled with water.

P Q R S T U V W X Y Z

puff

1. A **puff** of smoke came from the chimney.
2. Running makes me **puff**.
It makes me breathe hard.
3. A powder **puff** is a soft pad used for putting powder on the face.

pull

Tony will **pull** Susy's sledge.
He will drag it after him.

pullet

A **pullet** is a young fowl.
A **pullet** lays small eggs.

pulley

The line is on a **pulley**.
A **pulley** is a wheel.
It has a hollow edge which carries the line.
A **pulley** helps to lift weights.

pump

A **pump** is a machine.
It forces liquid, air, or gas in or out of something.

This is a petrol **pump**.
It puts petrol into the car.

pumpkin

A **pumpkin** is a vegetable.
It can be made into pies.

punch

1. The boys **punch** one another.
They hit one another with their fists.
2. We had cold **punch** to drink at the party.
It was made of fruit juice, sugar, and water.

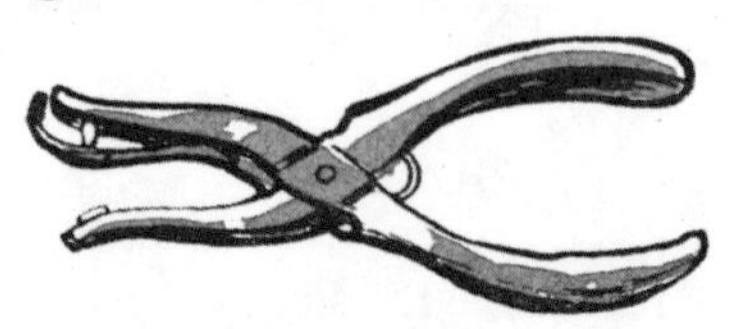

3. A **punch** is a tool used to make holes in paper.

P
Q
R
S
T
U
V
W
X
Y
Z

pursue, pursuit

Spot began to **pursue** Puss.
He began to run after her.
Scrappy joined the **pursuit**.
He joined the chase.

push

Ann likes
to **push** the baby pram.
She makes it go ahead of her.

puss, pussy

These are words for cat.

pussy willow

The **pussy willow** is a plant.
It has soft grey buds.

put

Put the kettle on the stove.
Place it on the stove.

Q q

quality

Cloth is of good **quality**.
It is a good kind of cloth.

quantity

Laura has a **quantity** of
nuts.
She has a great number.

quarrel

Ann and Mary had a
quarrel.
They said angry words
to each other.

quart

This is a
quart jar.
A **quart** is a measure.
It is two pints.

quarter, quarters

1. The apple is cut
into four equal parts.
Each part is one **quarter**.

2. Fifteen minutes is a
quarter of an hour.

queen

The wife of a king is called a **queen**.

queer

The sky has a **queer** colour. It has an unusual colour.

question, question mark

Why are the leaves green? That is a **question**.
A **question mark** is put at the end of a written **question**.

quick, quickly

Beth is **quick**. She runs **quickly**. She runs fast.
The girls cannot catch Beth.

quiet

Jayne is a **quiet** girl.
She makes very little noise.

quilt

A **quilt** is a warm covering.
It is used on a bed.

R r

rabbit

A **rabbit** is an animal with long ears.
It likes to eat vegetables.

race

The boys are running a **race**.
The boy who runs the fastest will win the **race**.

rack

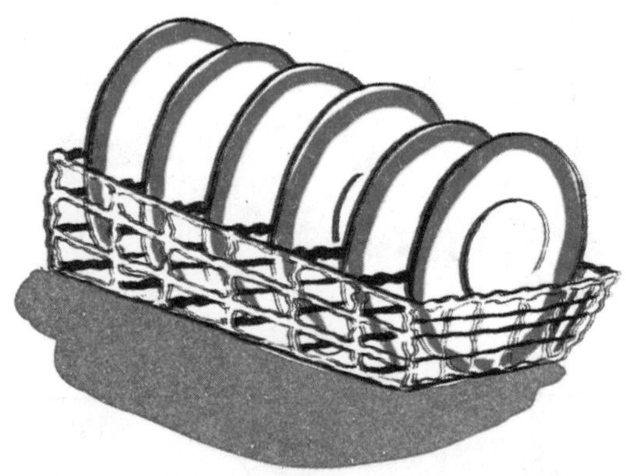

A **rack** is a framework on which things are put.
The dishes are in the **rack**.

radar

Radar is an invention.
By means of sound waves, an operator can tell where an object is, and how far away it is.

Q R S T U V W X Y Z

rain

Rain is water.
It falls in drops.
It comes from the clouds.

rainbow

The rain was falling,
but the sun came out.
Sunlight shining through
the rain made a **rainbow**.

raincoat

A **raincoat** is made of cloth
that can keep out the rain.

rainy

On **rainy** days, Judy
carries an umbrella.
She carries it on days
when it rains.

raise

1. Please **raise** the window.
Please put the window up.
2. Peter is going to **raise**
tomatoes in his garden.
He is going to have them
growing in his garden.

raisin

A **raisin** is a dried grape.

rake

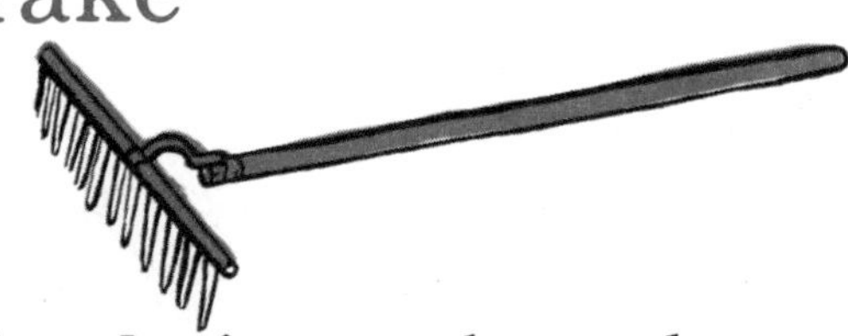

A **rake** is a garden tool.
One end is like a comb.
It has a long handle.
It is fun to **rake** leaves.

ranch, ranches

A **ranch** is a large farm.
Cattle are raised on **ranches**.

range

1. A **range** is a stove.
It is used for cooking.

2. People practice golf
at a driving **range**.

3. A line of mountains
is a mountain **range**.

ray, rays

A **ray** is a line of light.
The sun sends out **rays**.

rayon

Rayon is a thread or cloth.
It is made from plant material.

razor

A **razor** has a sharp blade.
Daddy shaves with a **razor**.

reach

The jam is out of Paul's **reach**.
He cannot **reach** it.
He cannot put his hand on it, because it is so high.

read

George can **read**.
He can look at the words and understand the meaning.

ready

1. Dinner is **ready**. Food has been cooked and served.
It is time to eat dinner.
2. Spot is always **ready** to play with us.
He always likes to play.

real

1. Alfred was a **real** king.
He once ruled over England.
2. The bag is made of **real** leather.
It is not made of other goods that look like leather.

really

Ben is **really** sorry that he lost the ball.
He is truly sorry.

reap

The men **reap** the grain.
They cut the grain when it is ripe.

R S T U V W X Y Z

reel

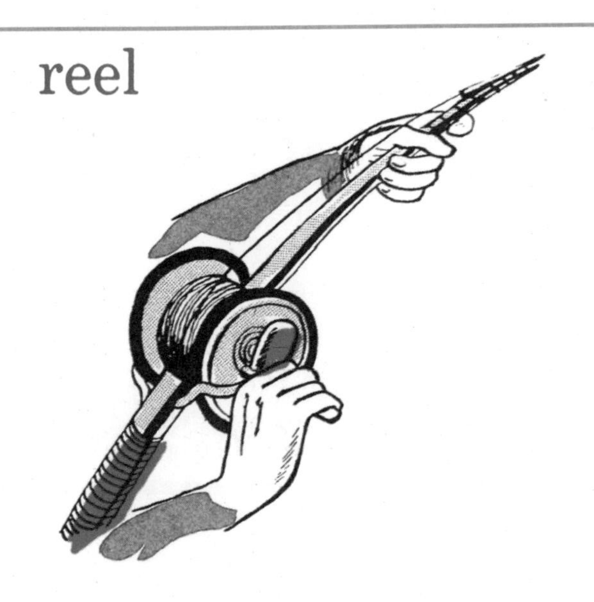

1. A **reel** is a spool.
Cord is wound on a **reel**.
The fishing rod has a **reel**.

2. A **reel** is a dance.

refer

1. Did Bob **refer** to the game?
Did he speak of the game?

2. What does the word mean?
Refer to the dictionary.
Look in the dictionary to find the meaning.

refrigerator

A **refrigerator** is a box in which food is kept cold.

refuse

Ruth had to **refuse** Virginia's invitation.
She had to tell Virginia that she could not come.

region

A **region** is a stretch of land.
It has a special use.
A forest **region** is covered with trees.

regular

1. Peter plants his beans in **regular** rows.
The rows are straight and even.

2. The school bell is **regular**.
It sounds at the same time every day.

remind

Remind Bob to post the letter.
Tell him to remember it.

remove

Ann will **remove** the dishes.
She will take them away.

rent

1. There is a **rent** in Dorothy's dress.
There is a tear in it.
2. **Rent** is money paid for the use of a house, a room, land, or the like.

repair

The man will **repair** the roof.
He will mend the roof.

repeat

I did not hear what you said.
Will you please **repeat** it?
Will you please say it again?

reply

Bob made a **reply**.
He made an answer.

report

1. The gun made a **report**.
The gun made a loud noise.
2. We heard the **report** of the fire on the radio.
We heard the news of the fire.

report card

Henry has brought home his **report card** from school.
The card tells his parents about his work and conduct.

request

Mother will **request** the lady to take off her hat.
She will ask the lady.

rescue

The barn was on fire.
The farmer was able to **rescue** his horses.
He saved them from danger.

reservoir

The **reservoir** is a big lake.
Water for the whole city is kept in the **reservoir**.

R S T U V W X Y Z

reward

Mandy has a medal.
It is a **reward**
for doing good work.
It was given to her
because she did good work.

rhyme, rhymes

Two words that end
with the same sound
are words that **rhyme**.
GAY **rhymes** with PLAY.
CREPT **rhymes** with SLEPT.

ribbon

Helen has a blue **ribbon**
to tie up her hair.
A **ribbon** is a long,
narrow band of cloth.

rice

Rice is a grain.
It is used for food.

rich

1. Mr. Jones is **rich**.
He has much money.
2. The soil is **rich**.
It produces good crops.
3. **Rich** food has much
fat or sugar in it.

rid

Puss will **rid** the house of mice.
She will drive them away.

riddle

A **riddle** is a question
that is hard to answer.

ride, riding, rode, ridden

When we **ride**, we are
carried by an animal or
vehicle.

We are **riding** in the car.

John **rode** on his bicycle.
Have you ever **ridden** on
an elephant's back?

rocket

A **rocket** is a firework.
It can be used as a signal.
When it explodes, gases
escape and force it
through the air.
The same principle can
be used to fly a plane.

rocker, rockers

A **rocker**
is a curved piece of wood.
The chair has two **rockers**.

rocking horse

Pete has a **rocking horse**.
It is a large toy horse.
It moves on rockers.

rod

A **rod** is a round stick.
It is straight and thin.
This is a curtain **rod**.

roll

1. See
Toby **roll** in the grass.
He turns over and over.

2. The boys **roll** up the rug.
3. A **roll** is
a small
piece of
baked
dough.

roller skates

Roller skates have wheels.
Dora has **roller skates**.

rompers

Baby wears blue **rompers**.
It is a play suit.

roof

A **roof** covers the top of a
building. The **roof** is red.

R S T U V W X Y Z

room

1. The chair has **room** for two.
There is space for two.
2. A **room** is part of a house.
It is set apart by walls.

rooster

The **rooster** is a fowl.
The **rooster** crows.

root

A **root** is part of a plant.
It grows underground.
The **root** takes food for the plant from the soil.

rope

A **rope** is a thick cord.

rose

A **rose** is a flower.
It grows on a bush.

rotten

The apple is **rotten**.
It has turned bad.

rough

Prince has **rough** fur.
It is not soft and smooth.

round

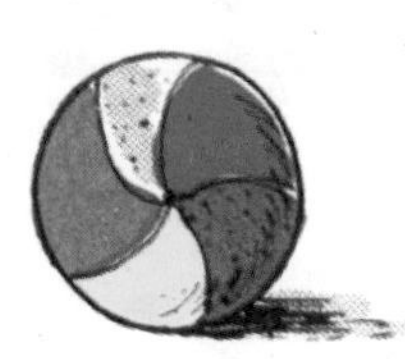

The ball is **round**.
It has a curved shape.

route

A **route** is the way taken from one place to another.

row, rowboat

1. A **row** is a line.
This is a **row** of plants.

2. See Edward **row** the boat.
He pushes the boat through the water with oars.
The boat is a **rowboat**.

ruler

1. A **ruler** is a stick used for measuring.
It is marked in centimetres and parts of centimetres.
2. A **ruler** is a person who rules a country.

run, running, ran

The horses **run** fast.
They are **running** a race.
One **ran** ahead of the others.
That horse has **run** faster.

rush

Mother asked Ann not to **rush**.
She asked Ann not to go so fast.

rye

Rye is a grain.
It is used as a food.
We make **rye** bread from this grain.

S s

sack

A **sack** is a large bag.
The flour is in the **sack.**

sad

Louise is **sad.**
She is unhappy because she has lost her dog.

saddle

A **saddle** is a seat.
It is made of leather.
It is used on a horse's back.

safe, safety

The light is green. It is **safe** to cross the street.
We can cross in **safety.**
We can cross without danger.

sand, sandy

Sand is stone which has been ground into powder.
The seashore is **sandy.**
Sand lies on the seashore.

sandal

A **sandal** is an open shoe.

sandwich

A **sandwich** is made of two pieces of bread with other food put between.

sash

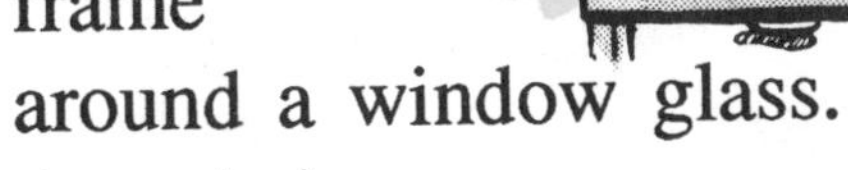

1. A **sash** is the frame around a window glass.
2. A **sash** is a ribbon tied around the waist.

satin

Satin is a kind of cloth.
It is made of silk.
It is shiny on one side.

sauce

A **sauce** is a liquid.
It is put on food to give it a better taste.

saucer

A **saucer** is a curved plate.
It is put under a cup.

sausage

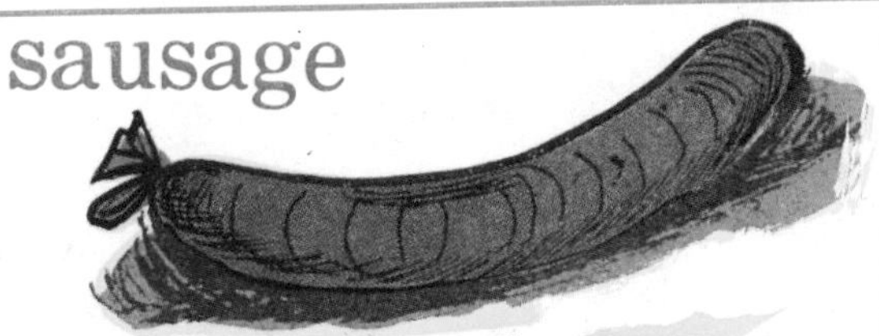

Sausage is ground meat.
Sometimes it is put into a covering of skin.

save, saving, saved

1. Jim likes to **save** money.
He keeps it for later use.
He has been **saving** all year.
He has **saved** several pounds.
2. Firemen **save** people from danger. Firemen get people out of danger.

seat

A **seat** is furniture on which we sit.
A chair is a **seat.**
A bench is a **seat.**

second, seconds

1. A **second** is a short time.
Sixty **seconds** make a minute.
2. Lena lives in the **second** house from the corner.
It is next to the first house.

secret

A **secret** is knowledge kept from other people.

secretary

1. A **secretary** is a person hired to write letters and to keep papers in order.
2. A **secretary** is a desk.

section

A **section** is a part.
Tom has a **section** of his aeroplane.

see, seeing, saw, seen

We **see** with our eyes.
The mind gets a picture of things at which we look.
We are **seeing** a ball game.
We **saw** Tom make a home run.
I have never **seen** a better game than this.

seed, seeds

A **seed** is part of a plant.
It can grow into a new plant.
These are **seeds.**

seek, seeking, sought

The boy went to **seek** his fortune.
He looked for a chance to make his fortune.
He was **seeking** work.
He **sought** it in the city.

seem

You **seem** happy.
You look as though you were happy.

sentence

1. A **sentence** is a word or a group of words.
It has a complete thought.
It may be a statement, a question, or a request.
2. A **sentence** is the statement of punishment to be given to one who has done a crime.

separate

A blouse and skirt are **separate.**
They are not joined together.

separate

Separate the small apples from the large apples.
Put the small ones here.
Put the large ones over there.

sergeant

A **sergeant** is an officer in the army or police force.

serious

1. Paul is a **serious** boy.
He is quiet and thoughtful.
2. Mary had a **serious** illness.
It was a very bad illness.

servant

A **servant** is hired to help with the work of the home.

serve

1. Father will **serve** the food.
He will give us our portions.
2. Bob will **serve** as captain.
He will act as captain.
3. This will **serve** me right.
It is what I deserve.

set, setting

1. **Set** the basket here.
Put the basket on the table.

2. Anna is **setting** the table.
She is putting dishes, silver, and napkins on the table.

settle

1. People came to **settle** here.
They came here to make homes.
2. The mud will **settle** at the bottom of the brook.
It will sink to the bottom.
3. The boys will **settle** their quarrel.
They will agree.

shall

1. I **shall** come with Grace.
We **shall** come early.
We are going to come.
2. Ben shall give me my ball.
He must give it to me.

shallow

The water is **shallow.**
It is not deep.

shape

Shape is the form of a thing.
The ball has a round shape.
The **shape** of the glove is like the **shape** of a hand.

share

1. The chocolate is for all of us.
Each one will get a **share.**
Each one will get a part of it.

2. Ann will **share** her umbrella with Dorothy.
The two girls will use it together.

sharp

The knife is **sharp.**
It has a thin edge.
It cuts things easily.

shave

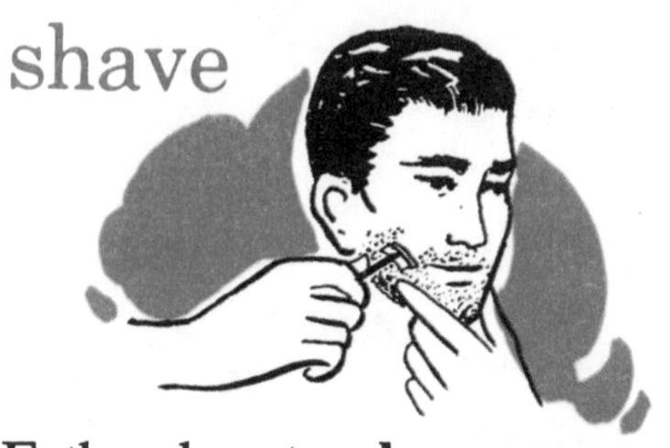

Father has to **shave** every day.
He takes the hair from his face by using a sharp blade.

she

Helen is going to pick berries.
She (Helen) has a pail.

shed

Some trees **shed** their leaves.
Their leaves fall off.

sheep

A **sheep** is an animal.
We get meat and wool from **sheep**.

S T U V W X Y Z

ship, ships

1. A **ship** is a large vessel.
It sails on the sea.
2. We **ship** goods on **ships** or trains. We send goods.

shirt

A **shirt** is clothing.
It is worn on the upper part of the body.
Donald has a blue **shirt**.

shiver

The wind made us **shiver**.
It made us shake with cold.

shoe, shoes, shoemaker

A **shoe** is a covering worn on the foot.
Most **shoes** are made of leather.
A **shoemaker** is a man who makes or repairs **shoes**.

shoot, shooting, shot

The hunter will **shoot** the gun.
He will fire the gun.
He is **shooting** at ducks.
He has **shot** one duck.

shop, shops

1. A **shop** is a building or room where goods are sold.
2. A **shop** is a place where things are made.
3. We **shop** for food.
We buy food at the **shops.**

shore

The **shore** is land at the edge of the sea.

short, shorter, shortest

1. The blue pencil is **short.**
It is not long from end to end. The yellow pencil is **shorter.** The red pencil is **shortest** of the three.
2. We waited for a **short** time.
We did not wait long.

silence, silent

There is **silence** in the room.
There is no noise.
Everyone is **silent.**
Everyone is quiet.

silk, silkworm

Silk is a shiny cloth.
It is made of thread spun by a **silkworm.**

silly

The story is **silly.**
It is a foolish story.

silver

Silver is a soft, white metal.
Some money is made of **silver.**
Silver is made into ornaments, knives, forks, and spoons.

similar

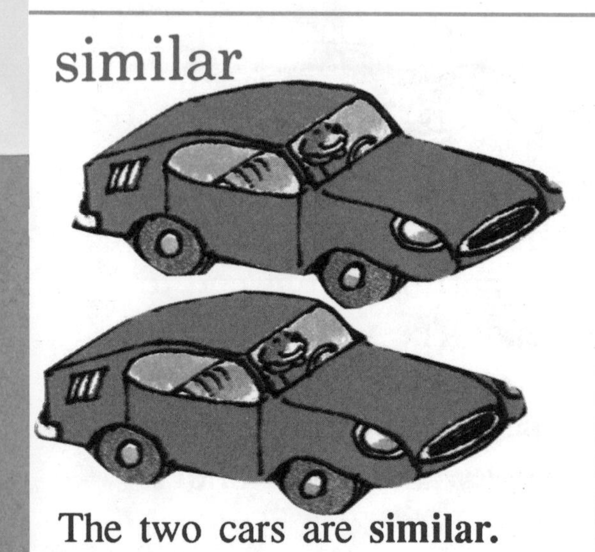

The two cars are **similar.**
They are alike.

simple

Making this hat is **simple.**
It is easy to make.

since

We have not seen Dora **since** school closed.
We have not seen her between that time and now.

sincere, sincerely

Jane's letter is **sincere.**
She writes **sincerely.**
She means the things that she has written.

sing, singing, sang, sung

We like to **sing.** We make music with our voices.
We are **singing** the song again.
We **sang** it once.
We have **sung** it twice.

single

1. The plant has a **single** flower. It has only one.
2. The flower is **single.**
It has one row of petals.

S T U V W X Y Z

ski, skis

We **ski** on the snow.
Skis are long, narrow blades that are curved at the front.
They are fastened on the feet.

skin

The **skin** covers the body.
Most fruits have a **skin.**

skip

1. A **skip** is a small jump.
2. Carol Ann likes to **skip** rope.
3. Do not **skip** any of the story.
Do not leave out any part.

skirt

A **skirt** is clothing.
It hangs from the waist.
Jayne has a yellow **skirt.**

sky

The **sky** is space above the earth. It looks blue.
We see the sun, the moon, and the stars in the **sky.**

slap

A **slap** is a blow with a flat thing or the palm of the hand.

sled

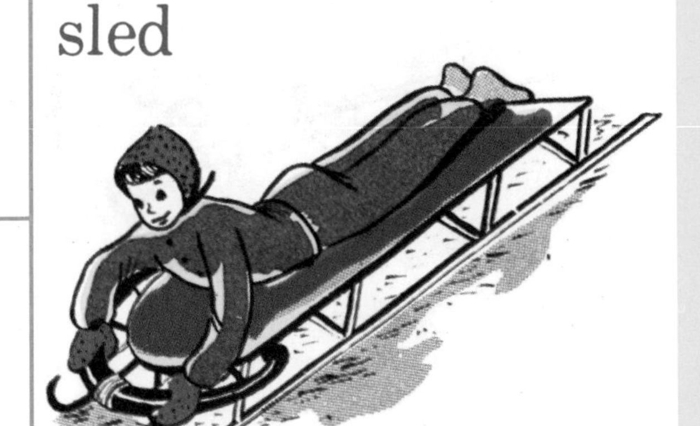

A **sled** is a vehicle. It runs on blades over the snow.
Barbara rides on her **sled.**

sleep, sleeping, slept, sleepy

We **sleep** at night.
We go to bed and close our eyes.
Sleeping gives the body rest.
I have **slept** for hours.
Mary Jane feels **sleepy.**
She feels like **sleeping.**

sleeve

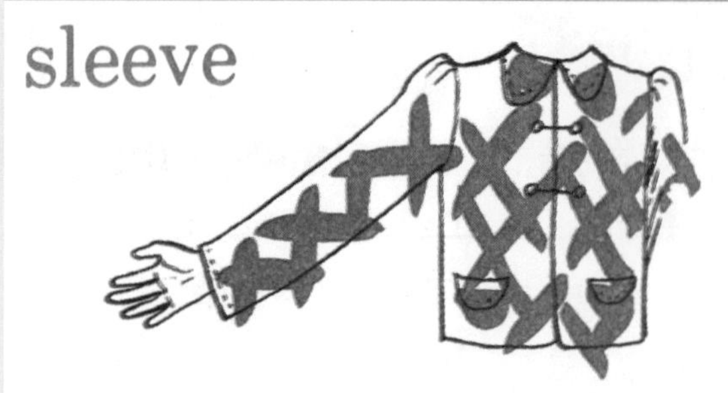

A **sleeve** is part of a dress or coat.
It covers the arm.

sleigh

A **sleigh** is a large sled.
It carries two or more people.
It can carry goods.

slice

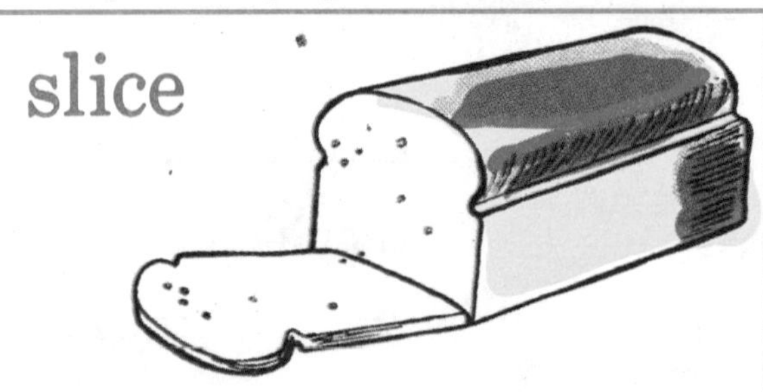

A **slice** is a thin piece cut from bread or meat.

slide

We **slide** on the ice.
We go over the smooth ice without lifting our feet.

slip

1. The ice made Donald **slip.**
His feet went from under him.
2. A **slip** is clothing worn under a dress.

slipper

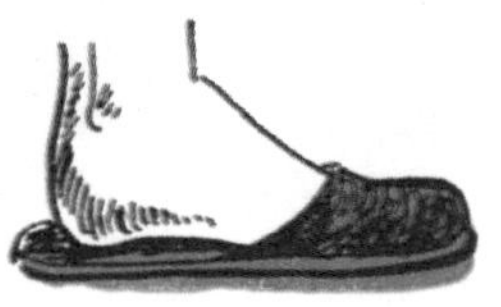

A **slipper** is a kind of shoe.

slippery

The floor is **slippery.**
It is so smooth that we could slip on it.

slow

That is a **slow** train.
It does not go fast.

small, smaller, smallest

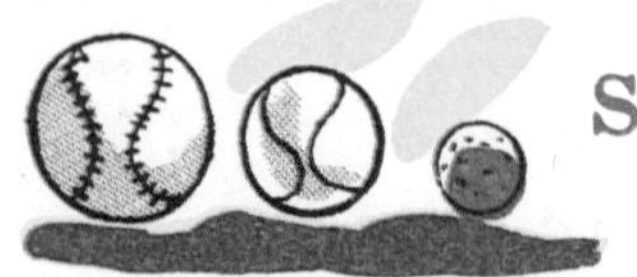

The baseball is **small.**
It is not large.
The tennis ball is **smaller.**
The golf ball is **smallest.**

snowball

Paul makes a **snowball**
out of the soft snow.

snowflake, snowflakes

A **snowflake** is a bit of snow.
If **snowflakes** were larger,
we could see that each
one has a beautiful shape.

snowman

This is the **snowman** that
we have made out of snow.

so

1. The moon is cold.
Dad told me **so.**
He said that it is cold.
2. It is **so** cold that people
cannot live there.
It is too cold for people.

soak

1. We shall **soak** the clothes
before we wash them.
We shall let the clothes
lie in water for awhile.
2. The rain will **soak** you.
It will make you wet.

soap

Soap is made of fat or oil
and other materials.
It is made into bars or
grains or flakes.
It is used for washing.

sock, socks

A **sock** is a short stocking.
It comes to the ankle or
knee.

sofa

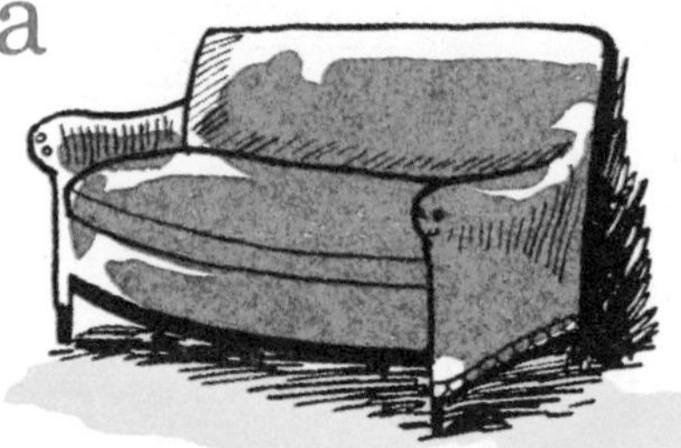

A **sofa** is a piece of
furniture.
It is a long seat.

soft

A **soft** thing feels smooth.
Pussy's fur is **soft.**

soon

The train will come **soon.**
It will come in a short time.

sore

My throat feels **sore.**
It pains me.

sorry

Jane is **sorry** that she cannot come.
She feels sad.

sort

1. What **sort** of bird is that?
What kind of bird is that?
2. We shall **sort** the nails.
We shall put nails of the same kind together.

sound

1. We hear **sound** when air waves are in motion.
2. The tree is **sound.**
It is a healthy tree.

soup

Soup is a liquid food.
It may be made of water and meat, fish, or vegetables.

sour

1. The apple is **sour.**
It has a sharp taste.
2. The milk is **sour.**
It is not sweet.

south, southern

South is a direction.
When we face the sunrise, **south** is on the right.
A **southern** place is a place lying to the **south** of us.

sow

Uncle Henry will **sow** corn.
He will plant the seeds.

space

1. There is **space** enough in the car for six people.
There is room for six people.
2. Leave a **space** between the plants.
Leave a place in which nothing is planted.

spade

1. A **spade** is a tool.
It has a blade and handle.
It is used for digging.
2. A **spade** is a kind of playing card.

S T U V W X Y Z

spider

A **spider** is a small animal.
It has eight legs.
It can spin a web.

spill

Do not **spill** the milk.
Do not let it run over the edge of the glass.

spin

1. We **spin** wool or other material by twisting it into thread.
2. See the top **spin!**

It goes around fast.

spinach

Spinach is a green vegetable.

splash

Martin made a **splash** when he jumped into the water.
The water went into the air.

splendid

The king wore a **splendid** crown.
It was covered with ornaments.

splinter

Jerry had a **splinter** of wood in his finger.
It was a small, pointed piece broken from a stick.

split

Uncle Henry **split** the wood with a blow of his axe.
He broke it into two parts.

spoil

1. The rain will **spoil** your hat.

It will damage your hat.

2. Put the meat into the fridge, or it will **spoil.**

It will not be fit to eat.

station

A **station** is a building at a place where trains stop.

statue

A **statue** is a figure made of stone, wood, or metal.

stay

1. In summer we **stay** at a hotel.
We live at a hotel.
2. **Stay** near the house.
Do not go far away.

steak

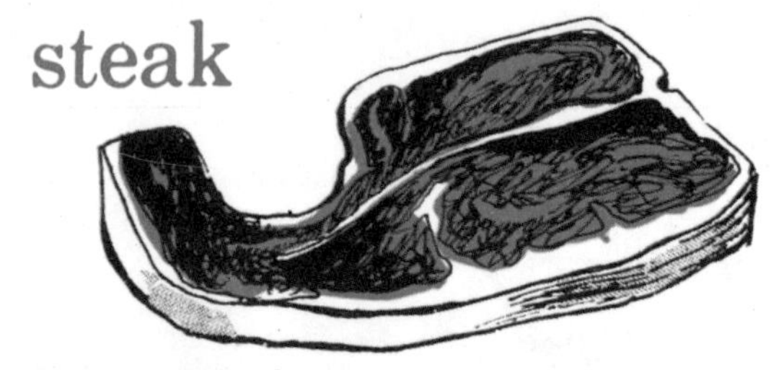

A **steak** is a piece of meat or fish.

steal, stealing, stole, stolen

Scrappy went to **steal** a bone.
He took what was not his.
We saw him **stealing.**
He **stole** a big bone.
We punished Scrappy because he had **stolen.**

steam, steamboat

Steam is a gas.
Boiled water turns into **steam.**
Steam is used for power.
A boat that is run by **steam** is called a **steamboat.**

steel

Steel is a hard metal.
It is made from iron mixed with other materials.
Tools are made of **steel.**
Steel is used for making bridges and buildings.

steep

The road is **steep.**
It goes uphill quickly.

steeple

A **steeple** is the tall part of the church building.

S T U V W X Y Z

sting, stinging, stung

1. A bee has a **sting.**
It has a sharp point.
2. It can **sting** you.
It can hurt you by sticking the **sting** into your flesh.
Bees were **stinging** Pat.
He was **stung** several times.

stir

1. **Stir** the pudding.
Keep it mixed by moving a spoon around in it.
2. Don't **stir** up trouble.
Don't cause trouble.

stitch

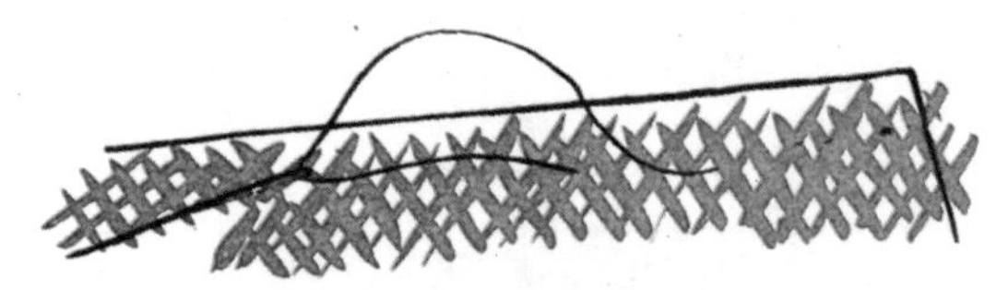

The needle and thread go through the material once.
That makes one **stitch.**

stocking

A **stocking** is a covering worn over the leg.
It goes up over the knee.

stomach

The **stomach** is part of the body.
Food that we eat goes into the **stomach**, where it is partly digested.

stone

1. **Stone** is a hard material.
It is part of the earth.
2. A diamond is called a **stone**.

stool

A **stool** is a small seat without any back.

stoop

Peter has to **stoop** to pull the weeds.
He has to bend over.

stop

1. Please **stop** shouting.
Do not shout any more.
2. We saw the car **stop.**
After coming down the street, it stood still at the corner.

S T U V W X Y Z

string

1. **String** is a thin cord.

2. A **string** is cord or wire on a musical instrument.

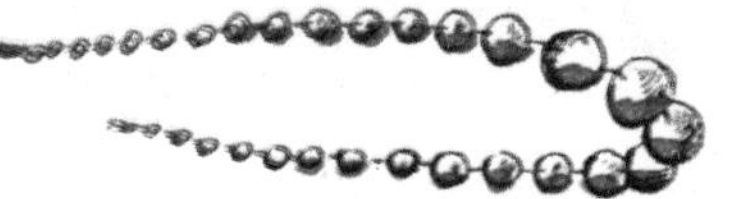

3. This is a **string** of beads.
The beads are on a **string.**

strip

1. A **strip** is a narrow band.
This is a **strip** of bacon.
2. Do not **strip** the bark from the tree.
Do not take it off.

stripe, stripes, striped

A **stripe** is a narrow band.
It has a different colour from the thing that it is on.
Jane's dress has **stripes.**
It is a **striped** dress.

stroke

1. Pussy likes us to **stroke** her back.
She likes us to move our hands over her back.
2. A **stroke** is one sound of the clock's bell.
3. A **stroke** is one movement of a brush or pen.

strong

Jack is **strong.**
He is healthy.
His muscles are firm.
He can play or work hard.

student

1. A **student** is a person who studies.
2. A **student** is a person who goes to school.

study, studying, studied

Grace will **study** her lesson.
She will give time and thought to learning her lesson.
She is **studying** history.
She has **studied** for an hour.

S T U V W X Y Z

stuff

We shall **stuff** the pillow.
We shall fill it with feathers.

stupid

The boy in the story was **stupid.**
His mind was slow.

style, stylish

Style is a way of doing things.
Stylish clothes are clothes in the best taste of the present day.

subject

1. A **subject** is a person who obeys a ruler.
2. The **subject** of a sentence names the thing about which a statement is made.
3. The **subject** of a picture is the person, thing or scene that has been painted.

submarine

A **submarine** is a boat that is able to go under the sea.

succeed, success

Jayne will **succeed** in art.
She will do well in art.
She will have **success.**

such

1. Have you ever seen **such** a dog?

Have you ever seen a dog of that kind?

2. We made **such** a noise that we awoke Grandmother.

We made so great a noise that she awoke from her nap.

sudden, suddenly

The storm was **sudden.**
It came **suddenly.**
It came quickly.
We were not expecting it.

suffer

People **suffer** when they are sick.
They feel pain.

sugar

Sugar is a sweet food.
It is made from **sugar** cane or from **sugar** beets.

S T U V W X Y Z

surprise

A **surprise** happens at a time when we do not expect it.

swallow

1. A **swallow** is a bird.
It can fly very fast.
2. We **swallow** food and drink.
We let them go down our throats.

sweater

A **sweater** is warm clothing.
It is like a shirt or jacket.

sweep, sweeping, swept

Judy will **sweep** the path.
She brushes the dirt away.
She is **sweeping** away dirt by moving the broom.
She has **swept** the path clean.

sweet

1. The fruit is **sweet.**
It tastes like sugar.
2. The flower smells **sweet.**
It has a pleasant smell.

swell

The bee stung Mary's hand.
Her hand began to **swell.**
It grew larger.

swift

1. A **swift** is a bird.
It lives on insects.
2. The horse is **swift.**
It runs very fast.

swim, swimming, swam, swum

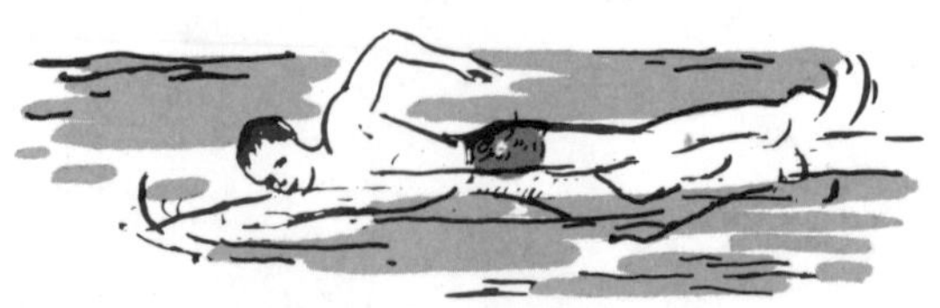

Jack can **swim** well.
He forces his body through the water with his arms and legs.
Swimming is easy for Jack.
He **swam** across the lake.
He has **swum** farther than that.

S T U V W X Y Z

swing, swinging, swung

1. Laura loves the **swing.**
The **swing** hangs from the tree and moves back and forth.
2. See Laura **swing** in the air!
Now she is **swinging** back again.
She has **swung** long enough.
Now it is our turn.

sword

A **sword** is a weapon.
It has a long blade.
It has a handle.

T t

table, tablecloth

A **table** is a piece of furniture.
It has a flat top and legs.
A **tablecloth** is a cloth used to cover a table.

tack

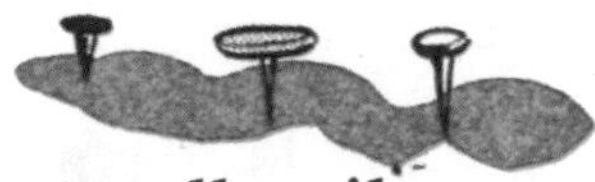

A **tack** is a small nail.

tag

1. There is a paper **tag** tied to the trunk.

2. **Tag** is a game.
One person runs after others.

tail

A **tail** is part of an animal's body at the end of the back.
The cow brushes off flies by moving her **tail**.

tailor

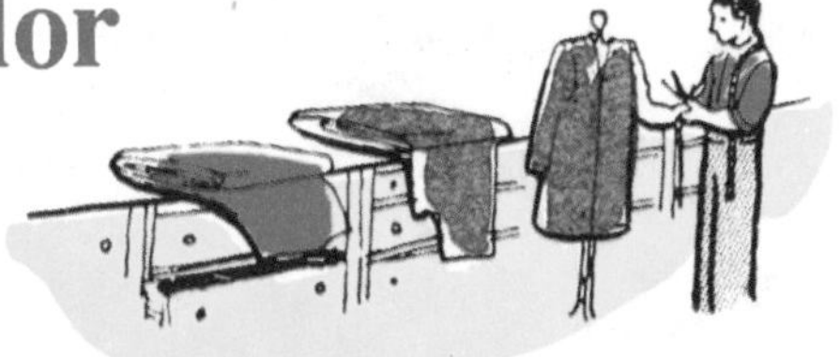

A **tailor** makes suits and coats.

taxicab

A **taxicab** is a car for hire.

tea, teapot

Tea is a drink made with water and tea leaves.
Mother makes it in a **teapot.**

teach, teaching, taught, teacher

Mr. Wells will **teach** us how to make a box.
He will show us how.
We shall learn from him.
He is **teaching** at our school.
He has **taught** us painting.
He is a **teacher.**

team

1. Two animals driven together are called a **team.**
2. People who play together in a game are a **team.**

tear

A **tear** is a drop that falls from the eye when we are sad or hurt.

tear, tearing, tore, torn

You will **tear** your dress.
You will make a hole in it.
The nail is **tearing** it.
It **tore** a small hole.
The **torn** part can be mended.

telegram, telegraph

A **telegram** is a message sent by **telegraph**.
Messages are sent to a distance by electric current.

telephone

By **telephone** we talk to someone at a distance by means of electric current.

television

Television is an invention by which we see things or people that are at a distance.
Light rays and electric rays are used in this invention.

T U V W X Y Z

thick

The red book is thin.
The blue book is **thick.**

thief, thieves

A **thief** is one who steals.
I read a story about forty **thieves.**

thimble

A **thimble** is a cover that fits over the finger of a person who is sewing.

thin

The peach has a **thin** skin.
The orange has a thick skin.

thing, things

A person is not a **thing.**
A place is not a **thing.**
Other objects that you can name are called **things.**

think, thinking, thought

George and Harry **think** that the camera is a good one.
They are **thinking** that they will buy it.
That idea is in their minds.
They have that **thought.**
They **thought** that the price was too high.

third

There are three ducks.
The first duck is walking.
The second duck is drinking.
The **third** duck is swimming.

thirsty

Jane is **thirsty.**
She wants something to drink.

thirteen

Thirteen is a number.
10 and 3 are 13.

thirty

Thirty is a number.
3 times 10 are 30.

through

The train
went **through** the tunnel.
It went from one end of
the tunnel to the other.

throw, throwing, threw, thrown

Let Pat **throw** the ball.
He sends it through the
air with his hand.
He is **throwing** it now.
He **threw** it high.
He has **thrown** it over the
house.

thumb

The **thumb** is
one of the fingers. It is
different from the others.
It is shorter and thicker.

thunder

Thunder is a loud noise.
It comes from the sky
after we see lightning.

ticket

A **ticket** is a card or paper.
It gives a person the right
to a seat in a theatre or on a
train.

tide

Tide is the rise and fall
of water in the sea.

tie

1. **Tie** up the package.
Wind string around it.
2. **Tie** the string in a knot.
Make it fast with a knot.

tiger

A **tiger** is a wild animal.
It is yellow and black.

tight

1. My shoe is **tight.**
It fits too closely.
2. The cover is **tight.**
It does not come off easily.

toe, toes

A **toe** is part of the foot.
A foot has five **toes.**

tomato, tomatoes

A **tomato** is the fruit of
the **tomato** plant.
It is good in salads.

tomorrow

Tomorrow is the day that
comes after today.

tonne

A **tonne** is a weight.
A metric **tonne** is 1000 kgs.
Coal is measured by the **tonne.**

tongue

The **tongue** is a long,
narrow organ in the mouth.
It is loose at one end.
We taste with the **tongue.**
We use it for talking.

tonight

Tonight is the night that
comes at the end of today.

too

1. The room is **too** hot.
It is hotter than it should be.
2. Get tea and milk, **too.**
Get milk in addition to tea.

tool

A **tool** is an object used
for working at something.

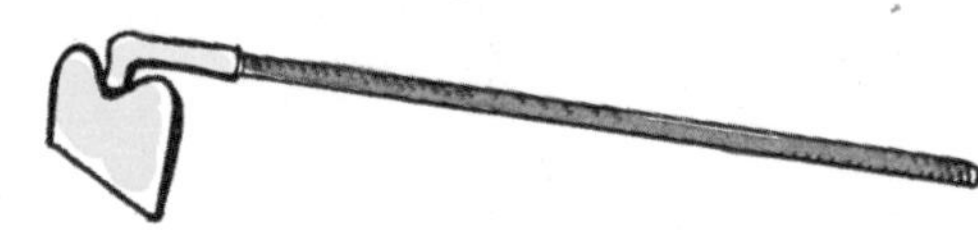

A hoe is a **tool.**

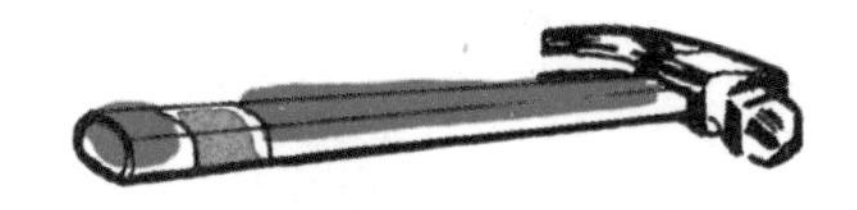

A hammer is a **tool.**

tooth, teeth, toothbrush

1. A **tooth** is hard and white.
It grows in the jaw.
We use our **teeth** for
biting and chewing.
2. A **toothbrush** is used
for cleaning the teeth.

3. A comb has **teeth.**

trace

We **trace** the map.
We put thin paper over it, and draw the map.

track

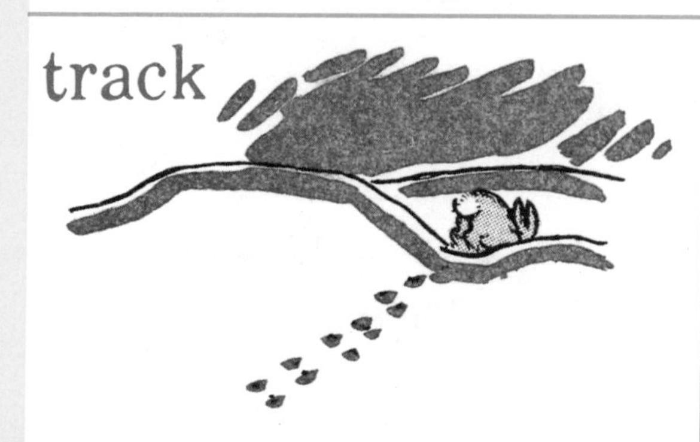

1. A **track** is a line of marks.
The rabbit made a **track.**
2. Trains run on a **track.**

trade

1. **Trade** is selling goods for money or other goods.
2. A **trade** is a way of earning a living.

traffic

Traffic means the coming and going of people and vehicles.

train

1. A **train** is a line of carriages.
2. We **train** Spot to beg.
We have him do it until he has learned how.

tramp

1. A **tramp** is a long walk.
2. A **tramp** is a person who goes from place to place.
He has no regular work.

travel

Andrew likes to **travel.**
He likes to go on journeys.

tray

We carry dishes on a **tray.**
A **tray** is flat.
It has a raised edge.

treasure

A **treasure** is a collection of valuable things.

treat

1. Doctors **treat** patients.
Doctors give them care.
2. The circus was a **treat.**
It was an unusual pleasure.
3. May I **treat** you to some chocolates?
May I get some for you?

tree

A **tree** is a plant.
It has a thick trunk and
many branches.
Leaves grow on the branches.

trial

The prisoner had a **trial.**
His story was heard in a
court of law by judge,
lawyers, and jury.

triangle

A **triangle** has three sides.

tribe

A **tribe** is a group of people.
A chief is their ruler.

trick

A **trick** is an action that
is hard to learn.
Spot has learned the **trick**
of carrying a newspaper.

trim, trimming

We **trim** the tree.
We put **trimming** on it.
We put ornaments on it.

trip, tripped

1. A **trip** is a journey.

2. Jerry **tripped** on the rug.
He caught his foot on it.

trot

Horses **trot.** A **trot** is a
way of running.

trouble

Terry is in **trouble.**
Things are not going
smoothly for him.
He is worried.

trousers

Trousers are
clothing
worn over
the legs.

tumble

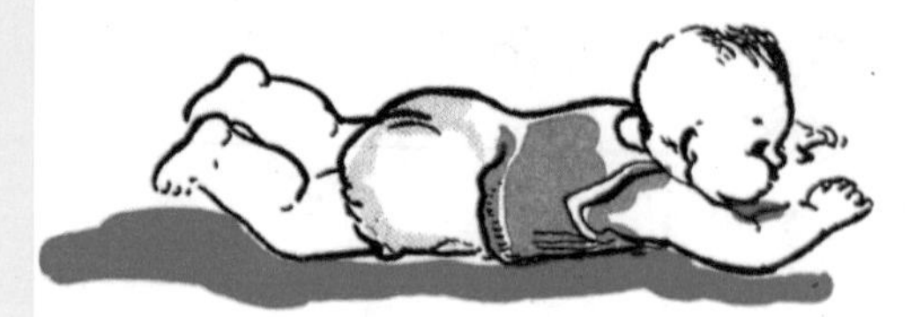

Baby had a **tumble.**
He had a fall.

tune

A **tune** is the music of a song.

tunnel

A **tunnel** is a way made through the earth.

turkey

A **turkey** is a fowl.
It is used as food.

turn

The merry-go-round will **turn.**
It will go around.

turnip

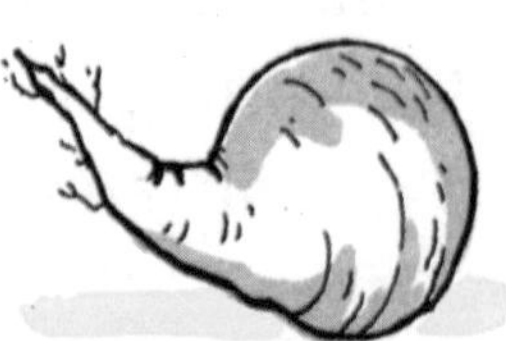

A **turnip** is a vegetable.
We eat the root.

turtle

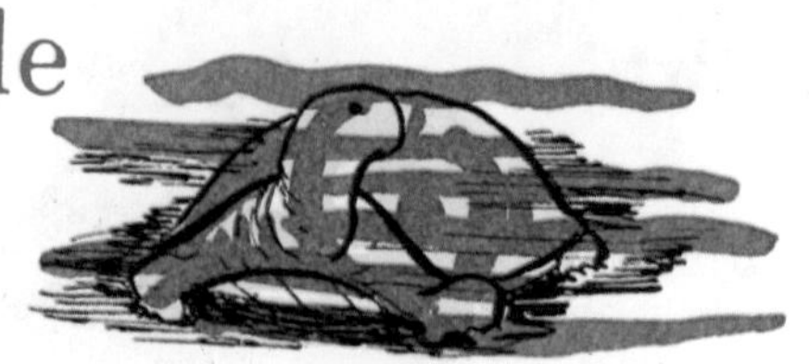

A **turtle** is an animal.
It has a shell.

twelfth

December is the **twelfth** month.
It is number twelve in order.

twelve

Twelve is a number.
3 times 4 are 12.
6 and 6 are 12.
The box has **twelve** eggs.

twenty

Twenty is a number.
4 times 5 are 20.
10 and 10 are 20.
We have 20 fingers and toes.

twice

Mother called once.
She called again.
She called **twice.**
She called two times.

T U V W X Y Z

twig

A **twig** is a very small
branch of a tree.

twins

Roy and Ray are brothers.
They are **twins.**
They have the same birthday.

two

Two is a number.
1 and 1 are 2.
We saw **two** ponies.

type, typewriter

Type is the form of a letter
that is used in printing.

A **typewriter** is a machine.
It has type for printing
when the keys are pressed.

U u

ugly, uglier, ugliest

One duckling was **ugly.**
He was not pleasing to see.
He was **uglier** than the
others.
He was the **ugliest**
duckling in the family.

umbrella

An **umbrella** is used to
keep off the rain.
It folds up when it is not
in use.

unable

The chicks are **unable** to fly.
They cannot fly.

uncle

Uncle John is Mother's
brother.
Uncle Henry is Father's
brother.

T
U
V
W
X
Y
Z

unload

The men **unload** the truck.
They take the goods out of
the truck.

untie

Ann will **untie** Baby's bib.
She will take out the knot
that holds it on.

until

We played **until** six
o'clock.
We played up to that time.

unusual

A comet is an **unusual**
sight.
It is not often seen.

up

The balloon went **up.**
It went from the earth
and into the sky.

upon

The vase is **upon** the table.
It rests on the table.

uphill

We are walking **uphill.**
We walk from the bottom of
the hill to a higher place.

upper

Charles
sleeps in the **upper** bed.
He sleeps in the higher bed.
It is above the other bed.

upright

1. The post is **upright.**
It stands straight up from
the ground.
2. The man is **upright.**
He is honest and fair in
all that he does.

upset

1. The basket is **upset.**
It has been turned over.
2. Ruth's stomach is **upset.**
It does not feel well.

upstairs

Laura goes **upstairs** to bed.
She goes up the stairs to
a higher floor.

up-to-date

The dress is **up-to-date.**
It is in the newest style.

uptown

We went **uptown.**
We went to the shops.

us

Ann and I received a gift
from Uncle John.
He sent it to **us.**
He sent it to Ann and me.

use, useful, used

Of what **use** is this tool?
What work can it do?
It is **useful** for raking
leaves.
It is **used** in that way.

usual, usually

It is **usual** for Tom to
forget his key.
He **usually** forgets it.
He does it nearly every day.

V v

vacant

The house is **vacant.**
No people are in it.

vacation

We had a week's **vacation.**
For a week we did not
have to go to school.
Dad had a **vacation**, too.
He did not go to work.

various

We tried **various** plans.
We tried a number of different plans.

varnish

Varnish is a liquid.
It is put on wood to give it a hard, smooth, shiny surface.

vase

A **vase** is an ornament.
It is hollow, like a jar.
The flowers are in a **vase**.

veal

Veal is meat.
We get it from a calf.

vegetable, vegetables

A **vegetable** is a food that comes from a plant.
These are **vegetables**:

peas

carrots

lettuce

beans

vehicle, vehicles

A **vehicle** is used on land for carrying people or goods.
These are **vehicles**:

cart wheelbarrow

car

truck

veil

A **veil** is thin material worn over the face or head.
Rose has a **veil** on her hat.

vein

A **vein** is part of the body.
It carries blood to the heart.

V W X Y Z

vinegar

Vinegar is a sour liquid made from apples or grapes.
It is used in cooking.

violet, violets

1. A **violet** is a flower.
2. **Violet** is a colour.
These flowers are **violet**.

violin

A **violin** is an instrument used for making music.
Grace plays a **violin**.

visible

Stars are **visible** at night.
They can be seen then.

visit, visitors

We shall **visit** Aunt May.
We shall stay at her house for a few days.
Aunt Mary likes **visitors**.
She likes to have people come to **visit** her.

vitamin, vitamins

A **vitamin** is a material found in certain foods.
Vitamins are needed to keep the body healthy.

voice

The **voice** is sound made by the throat and the mouth.
We use the **voice** for talking and singing.

volcano

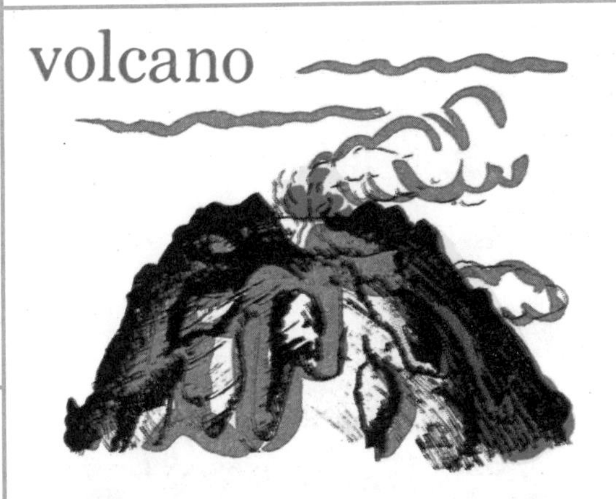

A **volcano** is a mountain.
It has an opening.
Gases and hot melted rock often pour out of the opening.

volume

1. A **volume** is a book.
2. A **volume** is one book from a set of books.

V W X Y Z

vote

A **vote** is an opinion.
People **vote** by raising hands, by speaking, or by writing.
They may **vote** by post.
People **vote** in an election.

voyage

A **voyage** is a trip.
It is taken on the sea.

vowel, vowels

a e i o u

A **vowel** is a letter.
There are five **vowels**.

W w

wade

We **wade** at the seashore.
We walk through the water.

wag

Pal will **wag** his tail.
He will move it from side to side.

wage

1. A **wage** is regular payment to a worker for his work.
2. Nations **wage** war.
They carry on war.

wagon

A **wagon** is a large cart.
It has four wheels.
It is often pulled by horses.
Donald has a small **wagon.**

waist

The **waist** is the middle of a person's body.
Ada wears a wide belt around her **waist.**

wait

1. **Wait** for Donald.
Stop until he comes.
2. There will be a short **wait** before dinner.
A short time will pass.

wave

1. Baby can **wave** his hand.
He moves his hand.

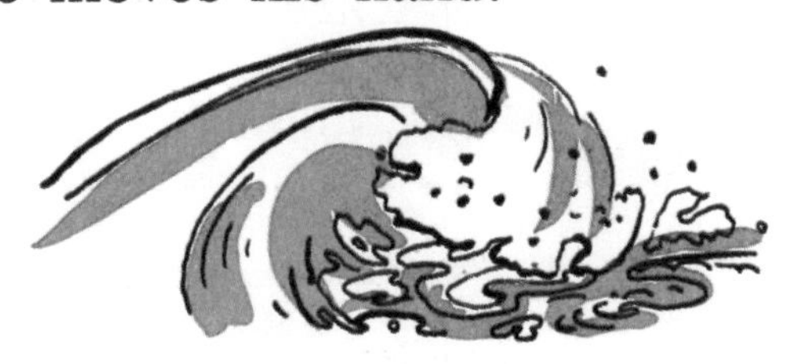

2. A **wave** is a mass of water that rises and falls on the surface of the sea.

wax

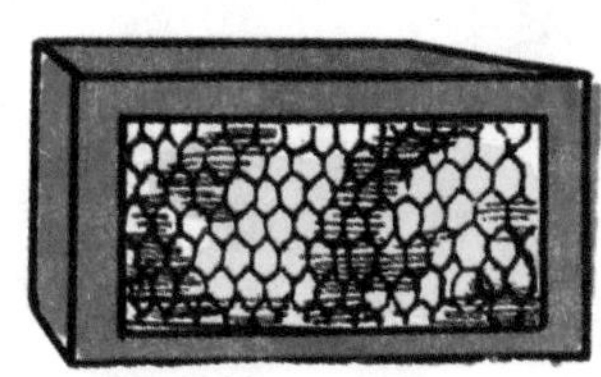

Wax is a soft material.
Bees make **wax** frames for storing their honey.
Candles are made of **wax.**

way

A **way** is a path from one place to another over the land or the sea.

we

Lois and I play together.
We (Lois and I) play cards.

weak

The puppy is **weak.**
It is not strong.

wealth, wealthy

Wealth is a great amount of money or valuable things.
Mr. Ellis is **wealthy.**
He is very rich.

weapon

A **weapon** is used for fighting.
It causes wounds or death.

A pistol is a **weapon**.

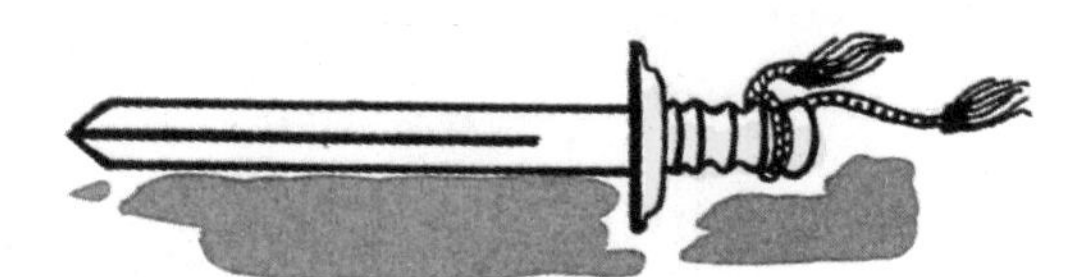

A sword is a **weapon.**

wear, wearing, wore, worn

1. Did Sally **wear** her pink dress to the party?
Did she put it on?
Yes, she was **wearing** it.
She **wore** it then, but she has never **worn** it to school.
2. The radio will **wear** out.
It is used so much that it will not be good any more.

weary

Mother is **weary.**
She is very tired.

welcome

We **welcome** visitors.
We show them that we are glad that they came.

well

1. A **well** is a deep hole in the ground from which we can get water.
2. The work is **well** done.
It is done in the right way.
3. Ralph feels **well.**
He does not feel sick.

went

We **went** away last summer.
We travelled to another place.

were

These trees **were** once small.
Now they are tall trees.

west, western

West is a direction.
The sun sets in the **west.**
Western places are places which are **west** of us.

wet

The road is **wet.**
It is covered with water.

what

1. **What** a crowd there was!
How great a crowd there was!
2. **What** play did you see?
Name the play that you saw.

whatever

We shall do **whatever** you think is wise.
We shall do anything that you think is wise.

wheat

Wheat is a grain.
It is made into flour.
The flour is made into bread.

wheel, wheels

A **wheel** is a round object.
Wheels are put on a vehicle.

The **wheels** turn around so that the vehicle moves.

wheelbarrow

A **wheelbarrow** is a vehicle.
It has one wheel, two legs, and two handles.
It is used for carrying things.

when

When does the parade start?
At what time does it start?

whenever

We shall go **whenever** you are ready.
We shall go at any time that you are ready.

where

1. **Where** is my hat?
In what place is my hat?
2. This is the place **where** we have picnics.
This is the place at which we have picnics.

wherever

Come out, **wherever** you are!
No matter where you are, it is time to come out.

whether

We could not decide **whether** to play ball or to play hide-and-seek.
We could not decide which game to play.

which

1. **Which** boy is Peter?
Is he the tall boy or is he the short boy?
2. That is a book **which** I have not read.
I have not read that book.

while

Helen listens to the radio **while** she studies.
She listens to the radio at the same time that she studies.

whip

A **whip** is a stick with a cord or piece of leather fastened to the end.
The man has a big **whip**.

wicked

The witch was **wicked.**
She was not good.
She did harm to others.

wide, wider

The sofa is **wide.**
It is **wider** than a chair.
It has more space from one side to the other side.

wife, wives

Rose and Andrew are married.
Rose is Andrew's **wife.**
The **wives** who live on her street play cards together.

wild

1. The tiger is a **wild** animal.
It is not friendly to man.
2. Some flowers are **wild.**
They grow in fields and woods.
They are not planted in gardens.

will

1. Joan **will** bring her book.
She is going to bring it.
2. I **will** finish this work.
I have made up my mind to finish this work.

willing

John is **willing** to help us.
He is glad to help us.

willow

A **willow** is a tree.
Its branches hang down.

wilt

Flowers **wilt** when they are not put into water.
They fade and die.

win, winning, won

Tony will **win** the race.
He will come in first.
He is **winning** easily.
He has **won** several races.

wire

Wire is a metal cord.
Wire carries electric current.
It has many other uses.

wise, wisdom

A **wise** person has knowledge.

He has **wisdom.**

A **wise** person is able to make right decisions.

wish, wishes

Grace has a **wish.**
She **wishes** to have a piano.
She would like to have one.

witch, witches

A **witch** is a woman mentioned in fairy stories.

Witches have magic power.

with

1. Jim is **with** Philip.
They are walking together.
2. Cake is made **with** flour.
Flour is used in making a cake.

within

Mother is **within** the house.
She is inside the house.

without

Allison came **without** a coat.
She did not bring her coat.

witness

Ted was a **witness** of the accident.
He saw the accident.

wolf, wolves

A **wolf** is a wild animal.
It is like a dog.
Wolves go about in groups.

woman, women

Mother is a **woman.**
Rose is a **woman.**
Women are adults.

world

The **world** is the earth and everything that is on it.

worm

A **worm** is a small animal.
It lives in the earth.

worry

Trudie has a **worry**.
Her mind is upset.

worse, worst

It was a bad fire.
It could have been **worse**.
It could have done more damage.
It might have been the **worst** fire in years.

worship

Worship is the love and respect given to God.

worth

The picture is **worth** a fortune.
It has a value equal to a great deal of money.

would

1. Sam **would** go if he were asked.
2. I told Tom that I **would** see that picture.

I had made up my mind to see that picture.

wound

A **wound** is damage done to a person or animal by a cut, blow, or shot.

wrap

Wrap the gift nicely.
Put paper around it.

wreath

A **wreath** is a circle of leaves or flowers.
There is a **wreath** hanging in the window.

wreck

When a ship is destroyed, it is called a **wreck**.

wren

A **wren** is a small bird.

wrinkle

A **wrinkle** is a fold in skin or material.
Grandfather has a **wrinkle** on his forehead.

wrist

The **wrist** is a joint where the hand joins the arm.

write, writing, wrote, written

Allison can **write.**
She can put words on paper.
She is **writing** a letter.
She **wrote** one yesterday.
She has **written** two letters.

wrong

The answer is **wrong.**
It is not correct.
It is **wrong** to tell lies.
It is a bad thing to do.

X x

x-ray

An **X-ray** is a ray of light.
It goes through solid bodies.
By means of an **X-ray,** doctors can see what is wrong inside a person's body.

xylophone

A **xylophone** is an instrument for making music.

Y y

yacht

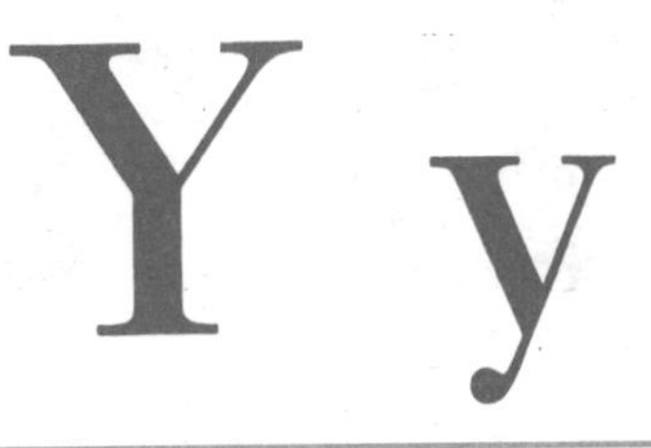

A **yacht** is a small sailing vessel used for pleasure.

yard

1. A **yard** is the space around a house.

We play in our **yard.**

2. A **yard** is a measure of length. Three feet or 36 inches make a **yard.**

yardstick

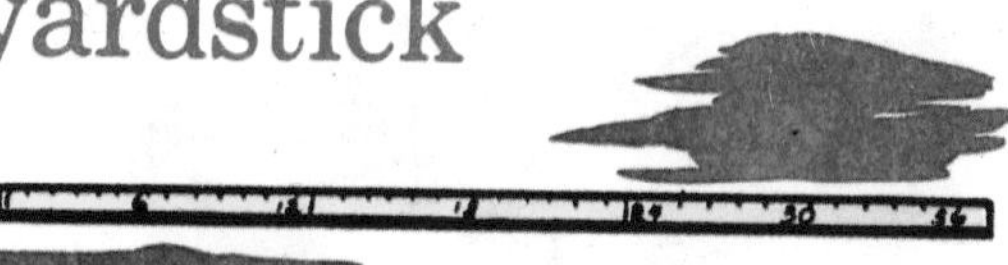

A **yardstick** is an old fashioned ruler.

It is a yard long. It is marked to show 36 inches.

yarn

Yarn is wool that has been made into thread.

yawn

We **yawn** when we are sleepy.

Our mouths open wide.

year

A **year** is a measure of time.

12 months make a **year.**

52 weeks make a **year.**

365 days make a **year.**

366 days make a Leap **Year.**

A Leap **Year** comes every four years.

yeast

Yeast is a material used in making bread.

It makes the bread rise.

yell

A **yell** is a loud cry.

It is made in pain or fun.

yellow

Yellow is a colour.

The taxicab is **yellow.**

yes

Did you study your lesson?

Yes. I did study my lesson.

yesterday

Yesterday is the day that came before today.

yet

1. The food is good; **yet** I am not hungry.

Even though the food is good, I am not hungry.

2. Dad is not home **yet.**

He is not home by this time.

3. We have **yet** more flowers.

We have even more flowers.

yoke

1. A **yoke** is a wooden bow put across oxen's necks to keep them together when they are working.

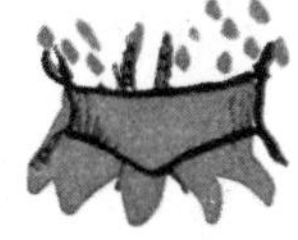

2. A **yoke** is the top of some dresses or skirts.

yolk

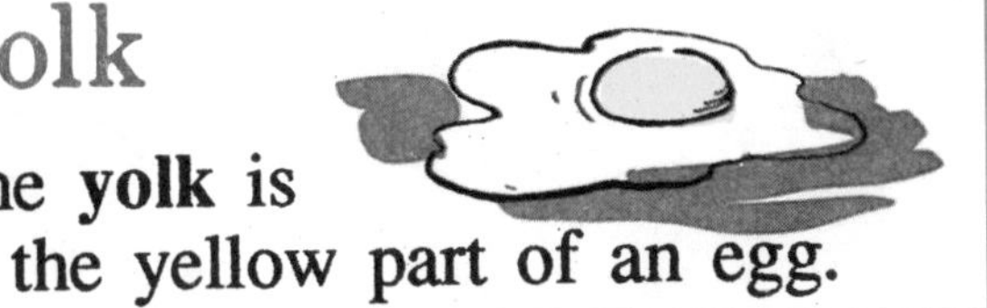

The **yolk** is the yellow part of an egg.

young, younger, youngest

Jayne is **young.**
She is only four years old.
Susy is **younger.**
She is three years old.
Baby is the **youngest.**
His age is one year.

you

Billy said, "I choose Jennie.
Jennie, I choose **you.**"

your, yours

This is Louise's book.
Louise, here is **your** book.
This book is **yours.**

yourself

You can see **yourself** if you look in the mirror.

youth

Youth is the time when a person is young.

Z z

zebra

A **zebra** is an animal.
It is like a horse.
It has stripes on its body.

zero

1. **Zero** is a number.
It means nothing.
2. **Zero** is a point on the thermometer. **Zero** is cold.

zinnia

A **zinnia** is a flower.

zoo

A **zoo** is a place where animals are kept so that people may come to see them.